101 Facts You Should Know About Food

John Farndon

ICON BOOKS

Published in the UK in 2007 by Icon Books Ltd,
The Old Dairy, Brook Road, Thriplow, Cambridge SG8 7RG
email: info@iconbooks.co.uk
www.iconbooks.co.uk

Sold in the UK, Europe, South Africa and Asia
by Faber & Faber Ltd, 3 Queen Square,
London WC1N 3AU
or their agents

Distributed in the UK, Europe, South Africa and Asia
by TBS Ltd, TBS Distribution Centre, Colchester Road,
Frating Green, Colchester CO7 7DW

Published in Australia in 2007
by Allen & Unwin Pty Ltd, PO Box 8500,
83 Alexander Street, Crows Nest, NSW 2065

Distributed in Canada
by Penguin Books Canada, 90 Eglinton Avenue East,
Suite 700, Toronto, Ontario M4P 2YE

ISBN-10: 1-84046-767-3
ISBN-13: 978-1840467-67-3

Typesetting by Wayzgoose

Printed and bound in the UK by
Bookmarque Ltd, Croydon

Contents

John Farndon is the author of many popular reference books on a wide range of topics, including the best-selling Dorling Kindersley *Pocket Encyclopaedia* and the Collins *Children's Encyclopaedia*. His most recent books for Icon are *Everything You Need to Know: Bird Flu* (2005) and *Everything You Need to Know: Iran* (2006). He has been short-listed three times for the Aventis Science Book junior prize.

Introduction

Food is the one thing none of us can do without. Fortunately very few of us in the developed world ever have to. Yet strangely, in these times of plenty, food is talked about more and more. In the past, most people had very little choice over what they ate. Nowadays, we are genuinely spoiled for choice. Supermarkets provide a year-round cornucopia of foodstuffs from all over the world. Restaurants serve a bewildering variety of cuisines. TV chefs entertain us with a host of different dishes that we could make if we put our minds to it.

It seems as if, as the choice grows, we begin to question more and more if we are making the right choice. Maybe we should avoid food containing trans-fats because it's bad for our health? Maybe we should eat berries because they are rich in anti-oxidants that slow ageing? Maybe we should buy organic because it's good for the environment? Sometimes we even wonder if we should eat food at all, because it could be contaminated by bacteria that cause food poisoning or additives that cause cancer.

Faced with such a dilemma, you could, of course, simply give up and eat whatever you fancy on a day-to-day basis, and damn the consequences. But our choices do have consequences, not just for us and our health, but for the health of the world, too. The aim of this book is to arm you with 101 facts about food that will help you make an informed choice.

As you read, you may learn things, as I did when compiling the book, that might just make you rethink some of your choices.

The wealth of choice we have, for instance, comes at a cost. Someone has to grow our food. Someone has to supply it. Someone has to sell it. The choices we make have a profound effect on all parts of the chain that brings food to our tables.

On the day I finished writing this book, the initial report of a UK Competition Commission investigating the power of supermarkets was due. Early signs suggested that, despite worries, they could not find any real reason for thinking that the supermarkets were abusing their dominance of the food market. Supermarkets, with some justification, claim that they are only giving us what we want – a wide choice of cheap, convenient, tasty food all year round. The challenge is: if we want anything different – if we want our food produced in a different way – then it's up to us to make that choice clear.

January 2007

1. The food industry annually spends over £10.5 billion on chemicals to add to food and alter it

All food is, of course, chemicals, but processors add a vast range of extra chemicals, so-called additives, to food – and these additives have become a gigantic business. Today, there's barely a food you can buy that does not contain at least some additives. In his book *Fast Food Nation*, Eric Schlosser describes how the New Jersey Turnpike in the USA is lined by vast flavour plants which despatch carefully balanced chemical brews to give flavour to everything from takeaway pizzas to microwave curries.

On average, people in the developed world consume 6–7kg of chemical additives every year. Food processors sometimes defend the use of additives by saying that they are used to make food last longer and kill bacteria. In fact, barely 1% of additives are preservatives or antioxidants designed to prevent food going rancid. Around 90% are flavourings added to make the food more enticing, or, more commonly, to make up for natural flavour lost during the manufacturing process. Other chemicals are added to help the food survive processing, such as emulsifiers to ensure that oil and water stay mixed, and anti-caking agents to prevent powders sticking.

Most developed countries have a long list of 500 or so chemicals that can legally be added to food. Although some additives have familiar names like sugar and salt, many are known by complex chemical names, such as butylated hydroxyanisol, which mean nothing to those outside the additive business.

Since 1983, food manufacturers in the European Union have

been obliged to list additives on the label, using either E numbers or chemical names. Interestingly, as the public at last began to realise just what range of chemicals was being added to their food, E numbers acquired a bit of a bad name, especially as some proved to be responsible for allergic reactions in some people. So now most food-makers give chemical names in full instead of E numbers, meaning that most labels have long lists of mysterious chemical ingredients.

You might think, reasonably, that the labels list *all* the additives in the food. But you'd be wrong. Labels show only the 500 or so additives that have been approved for use. They don't show any additives that have *not* been approved for use. Flavourings – in other words, 90% of food additives – don't need approval, and so they aren't listed. Manufacturers argue that there are too many flavourings (over 4,500) to list, that they are used only in minute quantities, and that commercial secrecy is vital. In fact, the use of flavourings in food is legally controlled only if one is proved to be harmful and so banned.

The business of food additives is incredibly complex, but as a general rule, it's probably worth avoiding sodium nitrite, saccharin, caffeine, Olestra (a synthetic calorie-free substitute for fat), ace-sulfame K (a low-calorie artificial sweetener) and any artificial colourings. And, of course, excess sugar and salt are best avoided too.

2. The largest modern fishing trawler drags a net twice the size of the Millennium Dome in London

Everyone knows that fish are pretty good for you, especially fish rich in Omega-3 oils like sardines and pilchards. The problem is, our taste for fish has stimulated an industrial-scale fish hunt that is in danger of reducing many parts of the once teeming oceans to fish deserts.

Once the preserve of brave fishermen working local seas with only their instincts and the most basic equipment, fishing has become a global high-tech business. Huge boats work far from home using the latest detection equipment to locate shoals, and giant nets for hauling gigantic loads of fish from the sea. These boats have all the facilities aboard to preserve the fish and stay at sea for long periods.

The world's largest fishing vessel is the Norwegian-built Irish vessel the *Atlantic Dawn*. One hundred and forty-five metres long and weighing over 14,000 tonnes, it could hardly be further from the traditional image of the fishing trawler. Its gigantic nets can drag a volume of water large enough to fill London's Millennium Dome twice over. On each trip it can land over 7,000 tonnes of fish – enough to give every single person in Tokyo a good fish supper! Interestingly, the *Atlantic Dawn* was initially registered as a merchant vessel to get round the EU limit on Ireland's fishing capacity – which this boat alone boosted by 15%. After tense negotiations, Ireland's quota was raised by 15%, and the *Atlantic Dawn* was re-registered.

Big, high-tech fishing boats like these have had an enormous impact on global fish stocks. Annual fish catches have risen 500% in the last 50 years, reaching over 95 million tonnes in 2000. The result, according to the UN's Food and Agriculture Organization, is that 52% of all the world's commercial fish are 'fully exploited', 17% are 'over-exploited' and 8% are 'depleted'. But these bare figures hardly conjure up just how severe the situation is.

The Grand Banks of Newfoundland were once the world's richest cod fisheries, heaving with a seemingly boundless supply of this large and nutritious fish. After the big trawlers brought a brief surge in the Newfoundland cod catch in the 1950s and 60s, it began to plummet in the 70s and 80s. In 1992, the last cod was caught. Many people doubt if cod will ever be caught there again.

3. The contents of the average British shopping trolley travel 95,000 miles to get there

Barely a century ago, most of our food was grown locally, within 100 miles or so. Now food preservation and refrigeration techniques and a global food transport network mean that our food comes from all over the world. The distance that food is transported has escalated dramatically. It has been estimated that the typical contents of a British shopping trolley for the family have travelled over 95,000 miles – nearly four times around the world. The beans might come from Kenya or Peru, apples from New Zealand or South Africa, asparagus from Egypt, baby corn from Thailand and so on.

All this has meant an enormous increase in the choice of food available in the supermarkets at any time of year. Indeed, we can get pretty much any produce we want when we want it, for what's out of season in one country is almost certain to be in season somewhere else in the world – or at least, that's the argument. This argument, though, becomes less convincing when it becomes clear that refrigeration techniques mean that the imported 'baby' new potatoes you buy in winter were probably dug up close to a year earlier and then frozen; or when shops are filled with imported apples at the height of the local apple season. Often, the reason why food is brought such long distances has nothing to do with seasonal availability. It happens simply because it's cheaper for the supermarkets to buy produce in less developed countries.

But it's not simply importing from around the world that has increased the distance that food travels to reach our table. Not only do we travel further to buy our food now than ever before, but supermarket distribution systems mean that food is shipped huge distances around the country from central depots. Often even when food is grown locally, it's shipped hundreds of miles on to the supermarket's distribution centre, then hundreds of miles back to the local outlet. Between 1978 and 2000, the distance that food was transported by lorry within the UK more than doubled. Indeed, the food lorries of the major UK supermarkets pound up and down UK roads relentlessly, covering over 1 billion kilometres (well over half a billion miles) a year. Nearly 40% of the trucks on UK roads are carrying food, and the number is growing by the year.

4. One in three kids born in America in 2000 will develop Type 2 diabetes

In January 2006, the *New York Times* ran a series of articles called 'Bad Blood', highlighting the terrible epidemic that is now sweeping New York City with little publicity. This epidemic is not some infectious disease, not cancer, nor heart disease, but the blood sugar disease, diabetes. One in eight New Yorkers – over 800,000 people – now have the disease, which is so prevalent in areas like the Bronx and Brooklyn that people refer to it familiarly as 'getting the sugar' or 'sweet blood'. Although New York has been especially hard hit, diabetes is on the rise throughout America. The American Center for Disease Control estimated that one in three boys and two out of five girls born in the USA in the year 2000 will develop diabetes. Among Hispanic children the risks are even higher, with half of all Hispanic children likely to become diabetic.

In fact, the disease is increasing throughout the world – wherever Western diets and lifestyles have been adopted. Since the mid-1980s, the number of people with the disease worldwide has skyrocketed from 30 million to 230 million. China alone has 39 million diabetics, while India has 30 million. Experts fear that by 2020, 350 million people around the world could be diabetic.

There are many factors behind this dramatic and already tragic rise, but most experts agree that lifestyle and diet are central. The disease is clearly linked with obesity, and the increased availability of cheap, high-calorie food – especially junk food – plays a key part. Many experts link the rise in diabetes in America to the soaring consumption of sweeteners, especially high-fructose corn sweeteners, which are often present in fast food. Some studies indicate that corn syrup can hinder the body's ability to process sugar.

What is most disturbing is that nearly all of these new diabetics suffer Type 2 diabetes. Type 2 used to be called 'adult-onset' diabetes, because in the past it developed in only middle-aged people or older. Now people are getting it at younger and younger ages. Indeed, many victims are teenagers.

5. The smell of raspberry comes from the interaction of over 300 different chemicals

Smell plays an incredibly important part in our identification and experience of food. Indeed, when you put food in your mouth, a huge proportion of its distinctive flavour comes from its aroma. The taste buds in your tongue can tell the difference between just five basic tastes – sweet, sour, salty, bitter or 'umami' (savoury). But your nose can identify over 10,000 different aromas, and it's aroma that enables you to distinguish between the flavours of an apple or a pear, a lemon or a grapefruit.

Smell has always played a crucial part in identifying whether a food is healthy to eat or dangerous. It's a very ancient sense, with smell receptors in the nose wired directly into the brain. Remarkably, our noses work in pretty much the same way as an insect's antennae to distinguish between the aromas of different substances. It's partly by studying the humble fruit fly that American scientists Richard Axel and Linda Buck were recently able to solve the mystery of just how smell works – an achievement for which they won the Nobel Prize for medicine in 2004.

You might think that you get the smell of food by sniffing it. In fact, you get most of the smell when you put it in your mouth. Then aromas from the food waft out through your nose as you breathe out. As the aromas stream out, they pass over smell receptors inside the top of your nose, in an area called the olfactory epithelium. Here there are clusters of receptor cells.

These 'olfactory' cells work in much the same way as taste buds, but instead of five basic types, there are 350 or so. Different aromas stimulate different combinations of smell cells. As you go through life, your brain learns to recognise these combinations and the average person knows over 10,000.

Aromas are essentially molecules of chemicals emanating from the food as vapours. It's the combinations of chemicals that give a particular aroma. Three key chemicals in the aroma of a raspberry are propionic acid, ionone and ethyl acetate. By themselves these three chemicals smell nothing like raspberry. Propionic acid smells a little vinegary, ionone vaguely flowery and ethyl acetate like glue. But together they smell at least a little like raspberry. The full aroma, though, comes from over 300 chemicals, each wafting off the ripe raspberry. When you smell a raspberry, olfactory cells in your nose respond to each of these hundreds of chemicals, then send off signals to your brain. Almost instantaneously, the brain analyses the combination and gives you the full raspberry experience – a feat of chemical analysis way beyond even the most sophisticated machine.

6. It takes 5,000 litres of water to make 1kg of cheese, 20,000 litres to grow 1kg of coffee, and 100,000 litres to produce 1kg of hamburger beef

Food production is completely dependent on water. Indeed, 90% of all managed water is used for growing and processing food. Crops need water to grow; livestock need not only water to drink, but water for food plants. Most food processing involves huge amounts of water. But even so, the amount needed to produce different food products varies enormously.

According to the US Geological Survey, it takes just 3 gallons (around 11 litres) of water to produce a single serving of tomatoes, 6 gallons (23 litres) for a single serving of french fries or lettuce, 35 gallons (132 litres) for rice and 150 gallons (568 litres) for a loaf of bread. This compares to a whopping 1,300 gallons (4,921 litres) for a hamburger.

Producing meat is incredibly demanding in terms of water use. Not only do farm animals consume a vast amount of food themselves, all of which needs water to grow, they drink a lot too – and the whole business of slaughtering and processing meat also uses a great deal of water. It takes 1,000 times as much water to produce a pound of meat as to produce a pound of wheat.

According to the International Water Management Institute, those on Western meat-eating diets consume the equivalent of 5,000 litres of water a day, compared to 1,000 litres for those on largely vegetarian diets in developing countries.

The problem is that there's barely enough water to go around now, and in the future things are likely to be much worse. As the world's population rises, the need for food also escalates, as does our need for water. In twenty years' time, we will need about 25% more water around the world to grow sufficient food. Yet global warming may mean we actually have *less* water available than we do now. When you add to this the forecast that the world's cities will increase their water demands by 50% over the next twenty years, it becomes clear that we may not have enough water to grow all the food we need.

Since producing meat uses so much more water than producing vegetables, it makes sense to cut down on the amount of meat eaten around the world. Yet the world eats more and more meat each year as developing countries such as China switch to Western-style, meat-heavy diets.

7. McDonald's gives away over 1.5 billion toys every year

Fast-food corporations know that appealing to children is a sure-fire way of bringing in customers. Bringing in children brings in parents who bring in money. According to Eric Schlosser, the author of *Fast Food Nation*, nine out every ten American children between the ages of three and nine visit a McDonald's once a month – as they and their parents are drawn by the seductive combination of playground facilities and give-away or special-edition toys, as well as the food. Toys attract children who pester their parents who bring the whole family to buy a meal which, of course, costs far more than the value of the toy. Moreover, children drawn by the toys when young will probably keep coming back to eat the food even when they are adults – and have children of their own.

All the fast-food giants have forged powerful links with the toy industry, and none more so than McDonald's, which is thought to be the world's biggest toy distributor, giving away or selling billions of toys each year. Nearly all the major toy crazes of the last decade, from Pokémon to Tamagotchis, have been linked to fast-food advertising campaigns. A successful promotion can double or triple weekly fast-food sales – and by marketing 'collectable' sets, fast-food outlets encourage repeat visits by children anxious to complete their collection.

Just how successful this strategy can be is illustrated by McDonald's' 1997 Teenie Beanie Babies campaign. The year before, McDonald's had ordered 100 million cuddly Teenie

Beanie Baby toys, each of which might retail at up to $2. In April 1997 they launched their campaign, and it was an extraordinary success. In a normal week, McDonald's sold 10 million children's Happy Meals, but in one ten-day period during the campaign in which a Teenie Beanie Baby was given free with each Happy Meal, over 100 million were sold. Indeed, within that ten-day period, four meals were sold on average to every child within the target age group in the USA. Estimates suggest that McDonald's made $250 million of sales on Teenie Beanie Baby Happy Meals during this promotion. The staggering success inspired McDonald's to repeat the campaign the following year, with slightly less success, and the year after, with less success still.

8. In just ten years, Vietnam has made itself the world's second-largest coffee producer, growing fourteen times more coffee than a decade ago

Coffee is the world's second most valuable traded commodity after oil, and there are about 25 million coffee farmers. A decade ago, it seemed to have a bright future, with coffee consumption rising in the developed world, and new drinkers emerging in the less developed countries. Vietnam, encouraged by the International Monetary Fund and the World Bank, began a drive to make itself into a major coffee producer. A million Kinh people were resettled in Vietnam's Central Highlands to clear and work hundreds of thousands of hectares of rainforest for coffee. So successful was this drive that within five years, Vietnam had come from nowhere to become the world's second-largest coffee producer after Brazil.

The problem is that production now far outstrips demand. In 2002, annual consumption was around 105 million 60-kilogram bags. Annual production was over 115 million bags. And so a surplus has been building up each year. Interestingly, despite the explosion of coffee-shop chains such as Starbucks, Costa and so on, and the corresponding arrival of specialist coffees – from mochas to skinny lattes – coffee consumption has, if anything, declined.

The result is that world coffee prices have plummeted to their lowest level for a hundred years. You mightn't have noticed this when you buy your coffee because the corporate giants that control most of the world's coffee – Nestlé, Kraft (Philip Morris),

Folgers (Procter & Gamble), Sara Lee and Tchibo – haven't passed on these price reductions to their customers. Instead they're making gigantic profits and passing on the dividends to their shareholders.

Vietnam is now taking a quarter of its coffee plantations out of production, but the effects of this coffee glut around the world have been devastating for many coffee farmers. There are tragic stories of farmers and plantation workers in Central America being forced out of business – helping to fuel the waves of migration of Hispanic people to the USA. And besides the human tragedy, environmentalists are concerned because so many coffee plantations are in sensitive rainforest areas, and the prospect of vast swathes of coffee land being turned over to pasture or other uses is alarming.

9. A third of all the fruit and vegetables we eat contain pesticide residues

The abundance of inexpensive but perfect-looking fruit and vegetables we see in our supermarkets has come at a price. To produce such perfect specimens, farmers now use phenomenal amounts of pesticides to control weeds, insects and fungi that would interfere with the crop. Pesticide sales tripled around the world between 1980 and 1999. In countries like Italy and the Netherlands, farmers now apply over 10,000 kg of pesticides to every hectare of cropland each year.

Quite apart from the damaging effects on the environment and the people who use them – 20,000 farm workers are killed by pesticides each year – many pesticides linger on crops and are carried through onto the food we eat. This is especially true of fruit and vegetables, which are not processed before they are eaten. Some pesticides linger on the fruit or vegetable's skin and can be removed by careful washing. Others are absorbed into the flesh and so can't be removed by washing or cooking.

In the UK, the Pesticides Residue Committee estimated that over 40% of fruit and vegetables sold contain significant amounts of pesticide. The Food Standards Agency argues that none of the pesticides individually are usually present in levels known to be hazardous to health. But pesticides are very rarely used singly. Most contaminated produce contains a cocktail of pesticides applied to ward off a range of different pests, and no one really knows what effect this could have when consumed over long periods.

Doctor Vyvyan Howard of Liverpool University has shown that British people now have 300 to 500 chemicals in their body that were just not there 50 years ago. Dr Howard believes that this chemical cocktail is having substantial effects on our health and our bodies. He talks about the effect of exposure of babies in the womb to hormone-based chemicals called endocrine disrupters, which are widely used in pesticides. This, Dr Howard believes, may be the reason why many girls are going through puberty at younger and younger ages. He believes that pesticides may also be implicated in the doubling of breast-cancer rates over the last 40 years. Meanwhile, a UK government committee on toxicity believes pesticide residues in food may be the reason why men's sperm count is going down.

Sometimes people eat salads believing them to be the healthy option. They certainly look pure and fresh sealed in their neat cellophane bags. In fact, keeping lettuces looking this perfect is often achieved only by soaking them in pesticides while they are growing, then drenching them in bleach to kill germs once they are picked. A recent survey by the UK Pesticides Residue Committee showed that over half the lettuces bought at UK supermarkets had substantial pesticides, in some cases above legal maximums.

10. The world's most delicious, nutritious food disappeared 2,000 years ago

In the times of Ancient Greece and Rome, the food that every gourmet wanted was silphium from Cyrene, in what is now Libya. It was probably a member of the carrot family, slightly similar to the plant *Ferula assa-foetida*, prized today in Iran and India. People ate silphium leaves and stems like cabbage, or added it to sauces for its wonderfully pungent flavour. They used it too for its remarkable medicinal qualities, able to cure anything from flatulence to high fever. Silphium was also great, apparently, for toothpastes and perfumes. And it was, so they said, the ultimate aphrodisiac. Such was the demand for it that whenever a new consignment arrived in Rome, people would queue for hours and pay exorbitant prices. Unfortunately, the money that could be made was so great that Cyrenians would uproot the plants before they had a chance to seed. So by the end of the first century AD, this amazing plant was extinct.

As farming is becoming more and more globalised, so many more crop plants are becoming extinct. Some time in the last century, the herb pellitory, once widely used as a tea and a herbal remedy, became extinct. A grain grown by the Araucana Indians of Chile, called mango brome, was thought to have become extinct too, but a few plants were discovered in Argentina in 1987. Interestingly, in recent years, farmers in Peru have 'rediscovered' other ancient Inca plants, which could well have been lost. The kaniwa, kiwicha, and quinoa are all grain crops that thrive at high altitudes much better than the wheat, barley and oats brought by the Spaniards. The Peruvian government realised that by promoting their cultivation they might be able to combat the childhood malnutrition that had become all too common in the Andean highlands.

11. Changes in farming have cut levels of vital minerals in fruit and vegetables by up to 75%

You might think that fresh fruit and vegetables are always healthy. You might appreciate that processing can reduce their nutritional value, as can overcooking. In fact, changes in farming practice and food preservation and transportation can substantially alter the nutritional value of fresh fruit and vegetables. Recent research, for instance, shows that the vitamin content of fresh fruit and vegetables declines with the distance it travels.

Changes in farming practice have had, if anything, more impact than transportation. Soil regularly fed only with artificial fertilisers gradually loses some of its key chemicals. When Anne-Marie Mayer of Cornell University compared the vitamin and mineral content of fruit and vegetables grown in Britain in the 1930s and the 1990s, she made an astonishing discovery. She found major drops in levels of key minerals like calcium, magnesium and copper in vegetables, and in magnesium, copper and potassium in fruit. Similar comparisons have revealed even more dramatic declines. Zinc, iron and magnesium content were all significantly down. Indeed, the mineral content of British fruit and vegetables seems to have plummeted by up to 75% in the last half century.

Similarly, intensive farming of livestock seems to reduce its nutritional value. The meat of cows fed on grass has much more of the beneficial Omega-3 oils than meat of cows fed on grain, and much less saturated fat. Milk from cows reared organically, too, has now been shown to have higher levels of Omega-3 than non-organic milk. Organic milk is now the first organic product to be recommended by government agencies for its health benefits.

12. The UK market for probiotic yoghurts was worth a third of a billion pounds in 2006

People worried about 'digestive discomfort' have been persuaded to buy probiotic yoghurts and yoghurt drinks. The market for these products generated by companies like Yakult, Danone, Müller and Nestlé is now enormous. The idea behind these yoghurts is that the digestive system contains its own flora of bacteria which aid or impede digestion. The theory is that the balance between 'friendly' bacteria which aid digestion and 'unfriendly' bacteria which impede it can be upset by various circumstances, such as a course of antibiotic drugs, excess alcohol, stress, disease and other factors. Probiotic yoghurts are said to reintroduce friendly bacteria and thus restore the balance.

Besides reducing the chances of irritable bowel syndrome, these probiotics are being investigated for a range of other health benefits, including reducing the risk of colon cancer, lowering lactose intolerance, cholesterol and blood pressure, and improving immune function – all by aiding digestion. Research has not yet proved conclusive, but there are many who argue that the same health benefits can be achieved more certainly by eating a diet rich in fibre, which has the same benefits for digestion as are claimed for probiotics.

In the gut of healthy adults, 10–15% of bacteria are friendly. But when the diet is low in fibre, or high in fat, the population can become depleted. Professor Glenn Gibson, head of food biosciences at Reading University, says that only 8% of the UK population eat enough fruit and vegetables, for instance, to give their digestive system the fibre it needs to keep the bacterial flora in balance. Professor Gibson also points out that the acidity of the stomach means that very few of the friendly bacteria in yoghurt actually make it through to the gut where they are needed. Because of this, food companies are working on including 'prebiotics' in their products. While probiotics introduce live bacteria into the gut from outside, prebiotics feed the friendly bacteria that are already there. Because they survive cooking, prebiotics can be introduced into a much wider range of foods. Kelloggs has already launched prebiotic Rice Crispies, while other companies are selling prebiotic baby milk and flavoured prebiotic water. Fruit and vegetables contain these prebiotics naturally, but the feeling is that most people cannot be bothered to eat them.

13. 80% of ten-year-old American girls diet

Ironically, just at a time when vast numbers of children in Western nations are becoming overweight, many other children are becoming so obsessed about their body image that they go on diets, just like their parents. Recent surveys indicated that four out of five ten-year-old American girls have been on a diet, and children as young as six are dieting. Many seven-year-old girls are refusing to eat birthday cake because it contains too many calories.

In a survey of pre-teens in South Carolina, more than half of ten- to thirteen-year-old girls felt they were too fat and wanted to lose weight – and many said they vomited to do so. By the time they go to high school, two-thirds of young girls are dieting, and one in five is using diet pills. One Chicago pre-teen said her dieting began at the age of seven, when she looked at the girl sitting next to her on the bus. 'I thought my thighs were a lot bigger than hers. I was shocked because I thought I was fat.' Even boys are not immune to this, with one in four boys of the ten to thirteen age group on a diet.

Around America, millions of children are going on diets, afraid of being fat. This has very little to do with coping with rising obesity, and means that many children are developing eating disorders that threaten their health and growth. Even when it doesn't develop into serious and life-threatening disorders such as anorexia and bulimia, dieting in children can disrupt their growth at a crucial stage, as well as affecting their learning and performance at school. The problem is that children need to eat well to grow well, and dieting can significantly impede healthy growth. Children go through stages when they are chubbier, and a chubby child does not necessarily grow into an overweight adult. The problems with dieting for children can be so severe that many health professionals say children should never diet. They should simply eat a healthy diet relatively low in fats and sugar and high in fibre – and excess weight should be dealt with by regular (not obsessive) exercise.

To explain American children's obsession with dieting, some people have blamed the attention given by health professionals to the problem of obesity. These children, they say, hear messages that they are too obese and try to do something about it. But research has shown that this isn't so. The real reason why children, especially girls, are dieting seems to be because of the media images they receive of the need to be thin to be popular and successful, and because they imitate their parents. Today's American children, as children all around the Western world, have grown up in a diet culture. All around them they see adults dieting and counting calories, while the TV shows thin stars and models, and the message they get is clear: diet or be a loser.

Unfortunately, they aren't given sufficient nutritional information to enable them to eat healthily without getting fat, so they simply cut down on food. This not only leads to health problems, but ironically disrupts growth in such a way that they may actually get fatter. There's a widespread belief among children that 'calories are bad', but their knowledge of other aspects of nutrition is patchy.

14. The way fast food changes brain chemistry can make it as addictive as heroin

There's no doubt that Western nations are eating too much sugary and fatty food. Obesity and diabetes are both at unprecedented levels. We recognise that for a few people over-eating is an illness they can't avoid, but assume that most people eat too much because they choose to and because the food is available. In recent years, though, neuroscientists have begun to wonder if there's more to it than that. What if, they are asking, food high in sugar and fat like junk food is actually physically addictive? If so, it would be as hard to cut down on junk food as it is to give up smoking or drugs like heroin.

Many scientists remain sceptical, but some research suggests that it's at least a possibility. One way in which junk food could be self-promoting is by neutralising the hormones that help keep body weight stable. One of these hormones, called leptin, is secreted by fat cells to keep the brain informed of the body's fat reserves. Unfortunately, as people gain weight, the brain becomes so used to high levels of leptin that it interprets any slight drop as a sign of starvation – and so tells the body to eat. One scientist observed such an effect in mice after just 72 hours of eating high-fat meals.

Sarah Leibowitz, a neurobiologist at New York's Rockefeller University, found in experiments on rats that fatty diets alter brain hormones so that the body seems to crave more fat. In particular, a high-fat diet seems to boost the production of galanin, a brain chemical that stimulates eating and slows down energy use. She found that when she fed young rats a high-fat diet for a while, they always became obese later in life.

Even more dramatic may be the effects of sugar. Addictive drugs are thought to exert their pull by hijacking the brain's natural 'reward' circuits – the parts of the brain that are squirted with pleasure chemicals like dopamine to give a sense of well-being. Most of the research in this field centres on how addictive drugs work, but some scientists are now wondering if giant doses of sugar can have a similar effect – stimulating the reward circuits to such a degree that any withdrawal of sugar intake is as uncomfortable as withdrawal from hard drugs. Indeed, one team of scientists testing rats fed with a high-sugar diet actually found the rats suffering chattering teeth, the shakes and anxiety when they were deprived of sugar – just like heroin addicts deprived of heroin. The idea that sugar is addictive in this way is still not accepted by the majority of neuroscientists, but research is under way.

15. Up to 4 million people in the USA are infected by salmonella food poisoning each year

Named after the American vet Daniel Salmon, who discovered it in pigs in 1885, salmonella is a bacteria found in poultry, unprocessed milk and in meat and water. It typically attacks the stomach and intestines, causing diarrhoea, stomach cramps, nausea and vomiting, headaches and fever. In minor cases, it simply causes diarrhoea for a few days, and requires no more treatment than rest and plenty of liquid. In more serious cases, especially in the very young and very old, it can be more serious, even fatal.

Salmonella is the main cause of food poisoning and affects maybe up to 4 million people in the USA each year. Worldwide, there are hundreds of millions of cases of salmonella infection annually. It's caught especially from chicken, raw eggs and food that has been poorly cooked or frozen, or not eaten soon enough. In March 2006, the US government estimated that 16.3% of all chickens were infected with salmonella. Some experts believe the figure is much higher. Many argue that this high incidence is caused by modern poultry rearing and feeding practices, in which huge numbers of chickens are kept in close proximity, allowing infection to spread easily.

Most cases of salmonella are individual and apparently unre-lated. Every now and then, however, there are major outbreaks attributable to a single source. In 1994, 224,000 people became ill in the USA from eating ice cream in a single outbreak. In 2005, Cadbury Schweppes was forced to recall more than a million of its chocolate bars after a number of them were found to be infected with salmonella.

In the UK and USA, hen vaccination programmes have cut the risk of catching salmonella from home-grown eggs substantially, but there is still a significant risk of infection from imported eggs. Moreover, there are hundreds of different variations of the salmonella bacteria, and they constantly mutate. So vaccinations that are effective against one variety may prove ineffectual against others.

16. Natural chemicals found in onions and garlic may protect against cancer

Bioflavonoids are complex compounds found in many plants, especially citrus fruit. They are closely linked to vitamin C and enhance its effects. They are often trumpeted for their antioxidant effects, and because they inhibit histamine release are thought beneficial for inflammatory or allergic conditions. There are several hundred different kinds of bioflavonoid, many of which have been recognised for particular health benefits. The rutin in buckwheat, for instance, is thought to be good for haemorrhoids and hypertension. The anthocyanidins in berries are thought to be powerful antioxidants. One of the most interesting is quercetin, which is found predominantly in onions and garlic. Quercetin is thought to inhibit the growth of cancer cells, especially breast cancer and leukaemia. It's also thought to help in healing wounds and preventing cataracts.

17. Most people in the world lose their ability to digest milk when they're young

Although all baby mammals are fed on their mother's milk, they lose their ability to digest the milk sugar lactose when they're quite young. About 10,000 years ago, cows were domesticated. Most adults at the time could not digest the lactose in milk and so could not drink the cows' milk. A few could, though, and this gave them a tremendous health advantage. Milk and foods made from it, such as cheese, are rich in nutrients and energy. So those who could take dairy products grew much healthier and survived in larger numbers to pass on their lactose-tolerance genes to their offspring. There is some debate about how the lactose-tolerance gene emerged. Some believe it developed in several places, such as Sweden, where lactose tolerance is very high, while others think it developed from a single source in the Middle East about 6,500 years ago. However it arose, the result was that most people in northwestern Europe can drink milk and eat dairy products throughout their lives without any problems, with clear health benefits. About 1 in 20 northern Europeans are lactose intolerant, but the proportion rises to half for Indians, two-thirds for South Americans, over 90% for Chinese and 100% for American Indians.

Although most people in the world are lactose intolerant, in Europe such a small proportion are affected by it that it's regarded as a medical condition. It was first identified by the famous Ancient Greek physician Hippocrates 2,500 years ago. Lactose intolerance is caused by a shortage of the enzyme lactase, which breaks down milk sugar into two simpler forms of sugar called glucose and galactose so that it can be absorbed into the bloodstream. People deficient in lactase may feel very uncomfortable when they digest milk products. Common symptoms, which range from mild to severe, include nausea, cramps, bloating, gas and diarrhoea. Lactose intolerance is sometimes confused with cow's milk intolerance because the symptoms are often the same, but cow's milk intolerance is an allergic reaction triggered by the immune system; lactose intolerance is a problem caused by the digestive system.

18. The organic food industry is expanding by 11% a year

As worries about the way our food is produced have grown, consumers have been turning increasingly to organic produce whenever they can. In Germany, already Europe's largest market for organic food, sales are rising at 12% a year, and in the USA at 15–21%. In the UK, they are going up by 30% annually, and the signs are that they'll keep on rising. Sales of organic fruit and vegetables, organic meat and poultry and organic milk are soaring.

Organic produce still commands only a small proportion of the market – 2.5% in the USA – but it has become the most dramatic growth area in the food business. In the UK, two-thirds of people choose to buy organic food at least occasionally, four out of ten buy it at least once a month, and one in four buy it at least once a week. Significantly, what started off as a middle-class movement, criticised as a fad for the better-off, has now begun to find interest right across the board. A survey in August 2006 showed that 57% of people on low salaries bought organic food whenever they could.

Organic farming is now a massive business around the world, with a market of nearly £17 billion. The leading markets are North America and Europe, while the leading growers are Australia, with over 12 million hectares of organic farmland, followed by China (3.5 million hectares) and Argentina (2.8 million hectares). The amount of organic farmland in Europe is growing apace too, especially in countries like Austria and Switzerland, where over 10% of all farmland is now organic.

The staggering rise in demand for organic produce has meant that growers in North America and Europe simply cannot meet it. It takes at least eighteen months to convert a farm to organic standards, and the process can be awkward for farmers used to farming by other methods. As a result, much organic produce is imported, leading to questions about its 'green' credentials.

The organic pioneers promoted the idea of organic as connecting to local farmers and local produce grown in a small-scale sustainable way, and in countries like the UK, the rise in demand for organic produce has gone hand-in-hand with a rise in sales at farmers' markets and farm shops. But the soaring demand has also led supermarkets to use their massive buying power to pressurise organic growers to expand and generate products in a particular way. Many of the original independents are being priced out of the market, and others are becoming global businesses. The massive US organic giant Whole Food is now worth £2.7 billion a year, and in late 2006, it opened the world's biggest organic food store in the centre of London.

19. Avocados contain a special kind of sugar that helps prevent low blood sugar, so may be the ideal diet food

The avocado got its name from the ancient Aztec word for testicle, and acquired a salacious reputation as an aphrodisiac, which is no doubt why Spanish monks banned it from monastery gardens after the conquistadors brought it back from Mexico. Nowadays, it's enjoying something of a renaissance. This time round, though, nutritionists are focusing not on its romantic benefits but its health benefits. Avocados are now often included in that band of select foods dubbed 'superfoods' because of their special nutritional value (see Fact 81).

First of all, avocado is thought to be good for blood cholesterol levels, and so for protection against heart disease. It's high in fat, so is both filling and full of energy, but it's the right kind of fat: monounsaturated fats. Avocados are rich in fibre and in plant chemicals called beta-sitosterol, which both help lower cholesterol. Australian research showed that eating half to one-and-a-half avocados a day for just three weeks could significantly reduce levels of the 'bad' LDL (low-density lipoprotein) cholesterol while maintaining levels of the 'good' HDL (high-density lipoprotein) cholesterol. Some researchers predict that heart patients could cut their risk of heart disease by 10–20% and their rate of death by 4–8% by eating an avocado a day over three years.

Avocados are also thought to help protect against heart disease by lowering blood pressure. Bananas are often advocated for their blood-pressure benefits because they are rich in potassium, but avocados contain two-and-a-half times as much. They are also rich in magnesium, which is again good for blood pressure.

Some researchers argue that avocados can protect against certain kinds of cancer, supplying antioxidants to mop up the free radicals that are thought to be cancer-causing. Avocados contain more of the antioxidant vitamin E, plus three times as much of the antioxidant glutathione, than any other fruit.

Diabetes organisations often advise people with Type 2 diabetes to eat avocados, too. They believe that not only do the avocado's contents of monounsaturated fat and triglyceride help protect against the heart disease linked to diabetes, but its high fibre content counters many of the effects of diabetes, including regulating insulin levels.

And finally, recent research has shown that avocados contain a kind of sugar that helps prevent blood sugar levels from dropping. This isn't only good for diabetics, but may also make avocados the perfect diet food. People are often spurred to eat more carbohydrate-rich food as their blood sugar levels drop. If their blood sugar stays at normal levels, they won't feel the need to eat to raise it.

None of the benefits of the avocado are fully proven yet. But there is enough suggestive evidence to make it worthwhile for all of us to eat avocados more often.

20. The temperature of food affects its taste

In Chinese food, the idea is that it should be piping hot, because that is crucial to its flavour, embodied in the phrase 'wok hei', which means the 'breath' or essence of the combination of tastes imparted by a hot wok. In 2005 Belgian researchers at Leuven University confirmed just how the link between temperature and taste works. They identified microscopic channels in our taste buds, termed TRPM5, which seem to respond differently at different temperatures. Apparently, the higher the temperature, the more intense the flavour is. This is why ice cream doesn't taste that sweet straight from the fridge, which is why ice cream makers add stacks of sugar – as you can tell all too clearly when the ice cream melts. In a similar way, some bitter tastes, like tea, taste better when hot because they are more intense.

21. Drinking a little red wine could be good for your brain

In recent years, some neuroscientists have been singing the praises of red wine, or rather a key ingredient of red wine called resveratrol. Italian scientist Alessandro Cellini found that fish given high doses of resveratrol lived 60% longer, and when other fish died of old age at twelve weeks, these Methuselah fish still had the mental agility of young fish. Resveratrol seemed to protect the fish's brain cells against age-related decline. Similar studies show that resveratrol is an antioxidant, protecting cells by mopping up free radicals, while others show that it actually encourages nerve cells to regrow. One group of researchers even suggested that a glass or two of wine a day can increase neural connections seven-fold. It may even protect against Alzheimer's. However, before you hit the bottle, it's worth remembering that alcohol is a major brain toxin. Even quite small amounts of alcohol can slow your thinking, ruin your sense of balance, wreck your judgement and completely obliterate your short-term memory. Long-term heavy drinking shrinks the brain and leads to memory loss and mental disorders. And the fish who benefited from those high doses of resveratrol were on the equivalent of 72 bottles of wine day! A glass of red wine a day for women and two for men won't do any harm, but it's far from proven that it really will do you good.

22. Chicken breasts are often less than 54% chicken, and may even contain pork or beef

You might think when you order a breast of chicken in a restaurant, or buy it in a supermarket, that it's simple, unadulterated chicken meat you are getting. But this is often very far from the case. When the UK Food Standards Agency investigated Dutch chicken breasts sold to a huge range of restaurants and other catering establishments, they found that the breasts were only 54% chicken. Besides huge amounts of water, this so-called fresh meat was full of added sugars, gums, flavourings, aromas and other additives designed to help hold all that water in.

Experts estimate that perhaps up to 15% water needs to be added to chicken to keep it moist during cooking. Water content above this is essentially to add weight and value. To get the chicken to retain a lot of extra water, however, processors have to inject the meat with additives. In the past, this used to be phosphates. Now it's more likely to be hydrolysed proteins.

Hydrolysed proteins are made from the unwanted parts of a carcass – skin, hide, bone, ligaments and so on. The proteins are extracted using high temperatures or hydrolysis, then added to the chicken to make it swell up and retain water. These proteins can come from other animals, not just chicken. You can sometimes tell that chicken has been adulterated in this way by its slightly spongy texture.

In her book *Not on the Label*, the *Guardian* journalist Felicity Lawrence describes how the UK Food Standards Agency became worried that if the protein injected into chicken came from cows, it could be infected with BSE (mad cow disease). After an investigation, they decided there was no evidence that chicken was being adulterated with beef waste. A BBC *Panorama* team began secret filming in meat-processing factories and found that in fact beef waste was being added to chicken in significant quantities. What's more, food company executives were boasting that they'd found a way of disguising the DNA of the added protein so that its origin was undetectable. *Panorama* found that at least twelve companies in Holland were using these undetectable hydrolysed proteins.

As a result, the Food Standards Agency is now lobbying the European Union to make the use of hydrolysed protein illegal, and to limit the permitted water content of chicken to 15%. At the moment, though, the chances are that chicken is being adulterated like this all around the world.

23. Studies in Australia suggest that over half the profit of big supermarkets comes from 'contributions' from suppliers

The enormous buying power of the big supermarket chains means that they have what is a stranglehold over many food suppliers. Supermarkets have lists of suppliers that they buy from, and the consequences for a supplier of being taken off the list are so severe financially that they bend over backwards to stay on it.

Pressure from the supermarkets means that suppliers have to supply things exactly as the supermarkets want them. The dimensions and colour of fruit and vegetables that growers can deliver is often specified to an extraordinary degree, with anything that doesn't come up to scratch being dumped. This has led to suppliers concentrating on fewer and fewer varieties of products such as apples, and growing them in a particular way so that they are the right size and colour, regardless of flavour. Organic produce doesn't fit well with this regimented approach, and suppliers providing supermarkets with organic produce have found themselves simply throwing away half or more of their crop because it doesn't quite match up. (See also Fact 28.)

For many suppliers, though, one of the worst aspects of their relationship with the big chains is the financial pressure. The consequences of being delisted are so severe that government investigations have found it hard to get them to talk about it openly. Yet it's clear that many practices go on which would surprise the general public.

For instance, the price war between the supermarkets that has been such a prominent feature of recent years is often funded by suppliers, under duress, rather than the supermarkets. When you see a discount in store, it's often the supplier that has cut costs, not the supermarket. Suppliers have to pay huge listing fees to get their products on the shelves and additional fees to pay for better positions on the shelves. It may cost a supplier hundreds of thousands of pounds just to get its product moved up a shelf. Whenever there are promotions or advertising campaigns, supermarkets demand a large contribution to the cost from their suppliers, even if the promotion is for an unrelated product.

One letter from Tesco has become a legend. Tesco, according to the story, requested a contribution from its suppliers towards the cost of its Dudley Moore TV advertising campaign for chicken. When a fish supplier from Cornwall received the request, he wrote back refusing. Tesco are said to have replied: 'Thank you, we will be deducting it from your monthly payments', and apparently did so.

Supermarkets are still massively profitable despite the cost-cutting wars between them, but much of these profits seem to come not from food sales but direct from suppliers. A study in Australia suggested that over half the supermarkets' profit came from direct payments made by suppliers. To meet these payments, suppliers have to cut ever more corners, and this makes itself felt both in the rock bottom wages paid to those working for the suppliers, and, inevitably, in the quality of the food. So the low prices in supermarkets may come at a cost.

24. Margarine enriched with plant sterols may help guard against heart disease

Plant sterols, or phytosterols as they are sometimes called, are natural chemicals found in plants. They are the plant equivalent of cholesterol, and play a role in the structure of plant cell membranes. In the late 1990s, scientists discovered that they are so similar to cholesterol that they can fool the body into thinking that they are cholesterol.

This is very useful, because they can masquerade as cholesterol and interfere with its uptake into the body in the digestive tract. Research at the Chicago Center for Clinical Research in 1999 showed that, consumed regularly, plant sterols can reduce concentrations of what everyone calls the 'bad cholesterol', LDL (low-density lipoprotein).

Phytosterols occur naturally in small amounts in vegetable oils, especially soya bean oil, which is why for a while soya was seen as a healthy food. Now many margarines, breakfast cereals and spreads are artificially enriched with plant sterols and marketed as health foods for those worried about high cholesterol levels. Such products are now big business.

In February 2005, Coca-Cola announced that it was going to launch a range of drinks fortified with plant sterols. In November 2006, scientists at UC Davis reported that twice-daily servings of a reduced-calorie orange drink with added plant sterols lowered levels of a chemical in the body called C-reactive protein. C-reactive protein is a sign of inflammation, and a well-known warning marker for heart disease. Professor Ishwarlal Jialal, the leader of the study, acknowledges that the best way to fight heart disease is through changes in diet and exercise. But, he says, people often can't make the necessary changes. Plant sterol-fortified juices may therefore be at least a help. This research was funded by Coca-Cola as well as the National Institute for Health.

Other scientists think the best way to use plant sterols is in pill form. They argue that taking them in fortified foods is unpredictable and erratic. It's impossible to be sure, for instance, when eating out, that the food is suitably fortified. Studies at Washington University in 2006 suggested that such pills could reduce LDL, but they are not yet approved for use.

25. More than a billion people around the world are classified as overweight; nearly a billion people are now malnourished

Nothing better illustrates the disparity between the haves and have-nots when it comes to food than this odd coincidence between the number of overweight in the world and the number who are suffering from lack of food. The grim reality is that there's enough food produced around the world every year for everyone to live on, but it's not equally distributed. Some people have far too much food; others have far too little.

There's actually a surplus of staple foods such as grains on the world food market. Every year, enough grain is grown around the world for everyone to have a kilogram every day. Some of this surplus is destroyed to protect prices. A great deal more is fed to cattle, pigs and poultry. Much of the food's nutritional value is wasted in this conversion to meat, which has of course become the dietary prerogative of the better-off countries, and the better-off in poorer countries.

Many Third World countries face severe environmental problems in growing food to feed their populations, such as drought, which is exacerbated by climatic fluctuations like those inflicted on the Sahel region south of the Sahara. But such problems are probably responsible only for less than a tenth of hunger-related deaths. Mostly to blame are human factors – notably transport and infrastructure, lack of investment due to debt, farm subsidies in rich countries that undermine the ability of farmers in poor countries to earn money from their crops, and the value added during processing, which makes it far more worthwhile for food suppliers to sell processed food to richer countries than basic foods to poor countries.

Nearly 815 million people around the world go to bed hungry every night, of which 300 million are children. Every five seconds or less, a young child dies of starvation, and another dies of diseases brought on by lack of the right food. Hunger and poor sanitation have killed nearly half a billion people in the last half-century, more than three times the number killed in all the wars of the last 100 years.

Back in 1996, governments got together at the World Food Summit and pledged to end world hunger by 2015. Since then progress has been almost non-existent, with worldwide malnourishment going down by just 2 million people each year. Many experts believe that the only way in which hunger and malnutrition can ever be really reduced is by a massive redistribution of wealth to the world's poor, including a complete cancellation of Third World debts, huge improvements to infrastructure in the Third World and a break-up of giant agribusiness farms into small family- and community-owned farms.

26. Beef consumption has risen 240% in China in the last ten years

The world is eating more meat every year. Rising affluence has meant that more and more people are turning away from traditional vegetable- and grain-based diets to eat greater and greater quantities of meat. Over the last half-century, world meat consumption has risen almost six-fold, from 44 million tonnes in 1950 to 262 million tonnes in 2005. On average, people now eat almost a kilogram of meat each week, and almost their entire body weight in a year.

Providing all this meat has led to a huge increase in the number of livestock on the planet. Today, we share the world with over 1.3 billion cows, 1 billion pigs, 1.8 billion sheep and goats and 13.5 billion chickens – that's over two chickens for each and every one of us.

But meat consumption varies tremendously across the world. The USA and China are the world's biggest meat-eaters. Between them, they consume over a third of the world's beef, half the world's poultry, and two-thirds of the world's pork. At least half of the rest is eaten in Brazil and Europe. People in the developed world eat almost three times as much meat – at 80kg – as people in the developing world.

In the developed world, though, meat consumption is beginning to level out. In the United States, it's even beginning to drop, thanks to concerns about the health effects of a meat-rich diet. But in the better-off areas of the developing world, particularly the cities, it's now rising rapidly. In the last five years alone, meat consumption in the developing world has soared by 24%, and the rise is accelerating.

The most dramatic rise is in China, as it becomes more affluent and more Chinese people are turning to meat-rich Western-style diets. China already eats half the world's pork, but what's most startling is the growth in beef consumption, which has much more than doubled in the last ten years and is expected to double again in the next five.

With China's huge population, the impact of this rising demand for beef will be massive. There won't be nearly enough rangeland for all the cattle needed to supply all this beef, so they will have to be fed on grain. Cattle are the most demanding of all livestock in terms of food. It takes seven times as much grain to produce 1 kg of beef as it does 1 kg of chicken. Calculations suggest that feeding the cows needed to provide beef for China alone will consume more than a third of all the grain now traded around the world each year.

In a world where so many people go hungry, the consequences of the surges in meat consumption cause heated arguments. Livestock already consume over 36% of the world's grain. Since continued growth of meat production will depend on feeding grain to animals, the world's wealthy meat-eaters are put in direct competition with the world's mainly vegetarian poor.

27. The biggest beneficiaries of the European Union's farming subsidies are not farmers but food manufacturers

For more than half a century, most governments in the developed world have paid generous subsidies to support their farmers and keep them producing food.

In recent years, such subsidies have come in for increasing criticism, especially from poor countries that find they are constantly undercut by subsidised producers in rich countries. Round after round of talks, first by the General Agreement on Tariffs and Trade (GATT), then by the World Trade Organization, have pledged to cut these subsidies. Yet, if anything, subsidies have increased rather than decreased.

You might think that the main beneficiaries of farm subsidies would be farmers, and critics of the European Union's notorious Common Agricultural Policy often paint a picture of rich farmers getting fat on handouts. In fact, by no means all food subsidies go to farmers. Besides paying direct subsidies to farmers on goods they produce, governments pay indirect subsidies to food traders to dispose of unwanted goods. Moreover, 'export support' is provided to traders who buy produce at a high price so that they can resell it cheaply on the world market.

The scale of export support is gigantic, and because food trading is largely in the hands of a few giant multinationals, these subsidies end up mostly in the hands of global corporations. Just four big US companies, Cargill, Dreyfus, ADM and Bunge – who between them control over 75% of US soya trade

– collected over $1.4 billion (£0.75 billion) in subsidies from the US government between 1985 and 1989. Meanwhile, the European Union paid out the bulk of its €1.5 billion (£1 billion) in export subsidies on sugar to just three giant multinationals – Cargill, Dreyfus and Tate and Lyle.

These giant companies are naturally very powerful lobbyists, and government officials wanting to try to reduce the scale of these massive subsidies to global corporations must often find their arms twisted. What's interesting is that the subsidies almost never go to fresh produce that fulfils basic food and nutritional needs. Instead, they go to the products that these companies handle, such as soya, corn starch and sugar, which are added to food to add value during processing. The result is that Western governments seem to be subsidising global corporations to give people the kind of high-fat, high-sugar diet which has led to the massive rise in obesity and food-related health problems in these countries.

28. Two out of every five beans grown go to waste because they're rejected by supermarkets

Naturally, vegetables and fruits grow in all kinds of different shapes, sizes and colours. Supermarkets, however, demand uniformity. For ease of packaging and marketing, they operate rigorous grading systems that accept only those fruit and vegetables that make the grade, and reject the rest.

The specifications for fruit and vegetables are surprisingly demanding. Size is a key criterion. Victoria plums for some supermarkets, for instance, must be exactly 38mm across. Green beans must be 95mm long and 5–7.5mm thick. Cox apples must be at least 65mm. Colour is another criterion. Some apples, for instance, make the grade only if their skins are exactly 15–17% red and 83–85% green. Beans and cucumbers must be straight as rulers.

For rejected stock, suppliers can at best hope to sell it cheaply for pulp. More often, because the supermarkets are pretty much the only real outlets, the rejects are simply thrown away.

The amount of wastage is huge. Around the world, maybe 40% of green beans grown each year are simply thrown away because they aren't uniform enough for supermarkets. In her book *Not on the Label*, Felicity Lawrence cites a carrot farmer who regularly throws away two-thirds of his carrot crop because it doesn't meet specifications.

Supermarket grading policies have more subtle effects, too. To make the size grade for apples, for instance, farmers have to push growth with fertiliser. The extra growth makes them less flavoursome. To reduce blemishes, farmers also have to use extra pesticides. To achieve the hardness that supermarkets require for good shelf-life, fruits may have to be picked early – so they aren't at their best in terms of flavour and sweetness.

Organic farmers in particular are hard hit by grading policies. With no artificial fertilisers to help promote growth, and no pesticides to control minor blemishes, they find that huge proportions of their crops are rejected. The ideal of sustainability that underpins organic farming is therefore lost as supermarkets take over the organic market – because so much of the crop has to be thrown away.

29. Replacing hydrogenated fat with natural unhydrogenated vegetable oils in processed food would prevent 100,000 deaths a year from heart disease in the USA alone

Trans-fatty acids or trans-fats are a type of unsaturated fat that are now provoking fierce controversy and major lawsuits. Small amounts occur naturally in meat and dairy products, but most of the trans-fats we eat come in the form of hydrogenated vegetable oils used in processed food.

Trans-fats are created when food manufacturers pump hydrogen through vegetable oil to create a solid fat, a process called hydrogenation. Hydrogenation is the difference between 'real' peanut butter that has to be stirred and smooth peanut butter that is uniformly creamy. The attraction of hydrogenated oil is that it can replace solid fats such as butter and lard completely, and survive even higher temperatures. The use of hydrogenated oils has meant that bread and other products can be baked at high temperatures in very short times. Hydrogenated oils are what keep crackers and biscuits crispy and cakes moist, and give baked products a long shelf life.

They were once thought to be better for you than saturated fats, but research has shown they are in fact, much, much worse. Not only do they raise levels of LDL (bad) cholesterol, but they also reduce levels of HDL (good) cholesterol. According to the Harvard School of Public Health, replacing hydrogenated fat in the American diet with natural unhydrogenated oils would save up to 100,000 early deaths from heart disease each year. The

American Heart Association recommends limiting daily intake of trans-fats to just 2.5g. That's just a few slices of bread or one or two biscuits a day, if they are made – as most are – using trans-fats.

Because of worries over trans-fats, the EU is investigating the possibility of a ban. Some supermarkets in the UK such as Marks & Spencer and Waitrose have voluntarily removed trans-fats from their products. Sainsbury's follows suit in 2007. In the USA, food products containing trans-fats sold in shops must be clearly labelled. There are no such restrictions on restaurants and fast-food outlets. In an effort to stop them using trans-fats, pressure groups in the USA have brought lawsuits against McDonald's and KFC. McDonald's settled out of court with a $7 million (£3.7 million) payment to the American Heart Association, but still uses hydrogenated oils. A large McDonald's french fries contains 8g of trans-fat. An apple pie contains 4.5g. A KFC potpie contains 14g of trans-fat.

30. Consumption of broccoli has risen 940% in the last 25 years in the USA

The main reason behind this astonishing rise in broccoli consumption is its fresh taste and convenience, and the success with which it fits into new, lighter styles of cooking. However, it's also a very healthy food, and is often included in the list of 'superfoods' (see Fact 81). It's low in calories and fat, and high in vitamins, minerals, fibre and disease-fighting substances – though only if eaten fresh and either raw or lightly cooked. It's high in minerals such as potassium, which help control blood pressure, and calcium, which guards against bone degeneration. It's also rich in the antioxidant substances that many people believe slow ageing and protect against heart disease, and in fibre, which protects the body against cancer and helps control blood sugar levels.

For similar reasons, carrot consumption has also risen, fitting well into the takeaway salads that are now such a common way of lunching. Of all the salad ingredients, it's the longest lasting and most colourful. Once the refuge of health fanatics, carrot juice too has become a popular drink, often called the 'miracle drink' for its health benefits. Carrot juice is one of the richest sources of vitamin A that can be used in the daily diet. It also ranks high as a source of the other vitamins, especially those of the B complex. Its mineral content is equally rich, and includes calcium, copper, magnesium, potassium, sodium, phosphorus, chlorine, sulphur and iron.

31. By 2007, 158 people in Europe had died of the disease vCJD caused by eating beef infected with BSE

Mad cow disease or BSE (bovine spongiform encephalopathy) has never killed as many animals as livestock diseases like foot and mouth, but it has attracted a great deal of attention because it's thought to be transmitted to humans in the form of variant Creutzfeld Jakob Disease or vCJD. It's a brain disease of cattle that was caused by bad farming practices. Since the 1950s, cows in Europe in particular have been fed 'concentrate' made from animal protein, often from other cattle or sheep. The cows have effectively become cannibals. Feeding on concentrate not only allows cattle to be reared more intensively; it allows the cattle, whose digestive system is used to breaking down tough cellulose, to bulk up quickly on easy-to-digest protein.

However disturbing in concept, the practice seemed to cause few apparent problems until the 1980s, when standards of preparation in concentrates were relaxed. Proteins found naturally in the nervous system survived processing in mutant form (prions) and were then ingested by cattle in concentrate. These deformed proteins erode the cattle's nerve cells, and cause other proteins in the nervous system to malfunction. The result is that prions spread through the cow, and from animal to animal, almost like an infectious disease.

As more and more cases of BSE appeared, millions of cattle in the UK were slaughtered. Exports of beef from the UK were banned and beef sales plummeted. It was feared that BSE was a timebomb as people who had eaten affected beef came to suffer vCJD. In 1996, the first British victim died of vCJD and since then 157 more have died in Europe, mostly in the UK.

In 2006, the epidemic was thought to have passed to the level at which all UK cattle could be sold for beef, providing they were properly tested. But many experts fear that BSE has by no means gone away, and there may be worse to come.

32. A 350g portion of 90% fat-free pie would give a woman over half her daily recommended fat intake

Most people in the Western world are very conscious of the need to limit the amount of fat, particularly saturated fats, in their diet. Figure consciousness and health are both powerful encouragements to keep fat consumption down. So for a long time now, foods have been advertised as 'low-fat' or even 'fat-free'. But just what does 'fat-free' mean?

You might think that fat-free means that a product contains no fat at all. Actually, it very rarely does. It simply means that it has less fat than the regular version. Usually, a product is advertised as 95% or 90% fat-free. This simply means that the fat content is 5% or 10%. A normal fat cake which is, say, 15% fat could be said to be 85% fat-free. The label 'reduced fat' means that the food just contains 25% less fat than normal.

Typically, with a product labelled fat-free, food producers are required to specify the fat content proportionally by weight. So in a product that's 90% fat-free, every 100g contains 10g of fat. So a 350g pie would actually contain 35g of fat.

The recommended daily intake of fat varies. It depends partly on whether you want to keep your fat intake down to stay trim, or simply to stay healthy. It depends too on your body mass index, and your lifestyle. Typically, though, the recommended daily intake of fat for women is about 60–70g. For men, it's about 90–100g.

So that 90% fat-free pie alone would contain more than half

the fat that a woman should eat in a day. What's more, the recommended daily intake of saturated fats is typically just 20g. So if a high proportion of the fat in that fat-free pie is saturated, it could easily put you well over the daily limit. In other words, you could find yourself eating far too much fat from just a single 'fat-free' pie a day.

Recommended daily fat intakes are often worked out as a proportion of your total food energy intake. It's thought that fat should provide no more than 35% of your food energy intake. Food energy is measured in calories, or rather kilocalories, and fat provides about 9 calories of energy per gram. So if you eat about 2,000 calories or kilocalories a day, you can work out that this should include 76g of fat. If your calorie intake is, say, 2,500, then you should have no more than 100g of fat a day.

In the UK, some food producers are labelling their produce with Guideline Daily Amounts (GDAs) which show how much the product contributes to your fat intake. In the USA, some are labelled with Recommended Daily Intake (RDI), and Daily Values (DVs). You can find out more about what this means on websites such as the British Nutrition Foundation (www.nutrition.org.uk) for Europe and the Healthguide (www.healthguide.org/life/food_labels_nutrition_facts.htm) for the USA.

33. Omega-3 oils may help to increase attention span and improve brain function

In recent years, a lot of people have talked about how oily, cold-water fish such as herrings are the ultimate brain food. Fish oil is rich in the fatty acid Omega-3, which is thought to have a wide range of benefits. Apart from being good for our physical health, including reducing the risk of heart attack and the joint pain associated with rheumatism, Omega-3 is now widely believed to contribute to our mental health, too.

Many scientists think it's a vital brain food at both ends of our lives. It plays a crucial part in the development of children's brains, for instance. A shortage of Omega-3 oil has also been linked to behavioural problems in children, and, controversially, the UK is thinking of introducing Omega-3 supplements for every British child.

When we get older, we might get depressed through lack of Omega-3, and our mental agility and memory may also suffer. Indeed, some scientists argue that Omega-3 is the key food in age-proofing your brain. A recent study of 4,000 older people in Chicago showed that among those who ate fish at least once a week, mental sharpness and memory declined 10% slower. Among those who ate two fish meals a week, it was 13% slower. The researchers likened it to knocking three to four years off your mental age.

Omega-3 is vital brain food partly because a form of Omega-3 called DHA (docosahexaenoic acid) makes up a significant portion of the membranes of neurons. It also encourages the production of BDNF (brain-derived neurotrophic factor), which helps promote new neuron growth and connections. And it plays a role in boosting the key neurotransmitters dopamine and serotonin – the decline of both of which are thought to contribute to brain ageing.

There are actually a variety of Omega oils besides Omega-3, including Omega-6. Omega-6 is sometimes portrayed as the 'bad' Omega oil, while Omega-3 is the 'good' one. Indeed, one of Omega-3's key benefits is to reduce the damaging impact of Omega-6. But it's not as simple as that. Omega-6, found in such foods as vegetable oils, eggs, poultry and cereals, helps to keep your skin healthy and your blood to clot properly.

What is needed is not all Omega-3 and no Omega-6, but just the right balance between them. The argument is that our modern diet has become swamped in Omega-6 with the increased use of vegetable oils in cooking and processing, while at the same time being starved of Omega-3 as we eat less oily fish.

34. 75% of the salt in our diet comes from processed foods

Health care experts have long drawn attention to the problems of eating too much salt. There is strong evidence that a diet high in salt can lead to raised blood pressure. Since high blood pressure is a major factor in coronary heart disease, it makes sense to cut down salt intake.

In the past, food contained very little salt, and people added it to their food at the table. Very few people add salt this way nowadays. However, the salt content of processed foods has gone up dramatically. It's now estimated that over three-quarters of the salt in the average diet in the developed world comes from processed foods, eaten without our being aware of it.

Salt is added to food partly to extend shelf-life, but more often it's dropped in to make up for flavour deficiencies created by the manufacturing process. This is especially true of ready meals and highly processed foods, but it's also true of such basic food as biscuits, breakfast cereals, soups and sauces, and even bread. Much mass-produced bread, for instance, contains so much salt – half a gram for every hundred grams of bread – that it's officially classified by the UK government as a high-salt food item. Salt has to be added to the bread because fast production time cuts the fermentation period in which flavour develops. Without added salt, the bread would taste like paper.

In the UK, the government has launched a drive to cut down people's salt intake. The UK Food Standards Agency argues that nearly half of the UK's population eat too much salt – 9.5g a day on average. Its aim is to bring down the average UK intake to 6g a day. The idea is to cut the salt content in 85 key food categories such as pizzas, bread, meat, cereals, cakes and pastries.

The campaign is having an effect. UK bread-makers have already cut the salt content of bread by almost a third, while cereal manufacturers such as Kelloggs have also made reductions. Kraft claims to have cut the salt in its Dairylea cheese spreads by a third. Major retailers such as Tesco and Asda also claim to have made significant salt reductions.

Nevertheless, the amount of salt we take in as we eat processed foods remains high. Foodsellers are not required to specify the salt content of food. However, they do often put the sodium content, and this gives an idea of how salty food is. Salt is about 40 per cent sodium, so to get the salt content, you simply multiply by 2.5. A food with more than 0.5g of sodium per 100g is high in salt. A 250g ready meal with 0.5g of sodium per 100g would contain 3.125g of salt, which is well over half what you should have in an entire day! It's not far short of a teaspoon of salt. It's better to choose foods with 0.1g or less of sodium per 100g. That way, you should keep your salt intake to a reasonable level.

35. 'Strawberry-flavoured yoghurt' may contain very little strawberry; 'strawberry-flavour' contains no strawberry at all

When you pick up a strawberry yoghurt, you might expect the flavours in it to come essentially from strawberries and yoghurt. That would be true if you made it at home, or on the farm. It's rarely true of commercial yoghurt, however. Most of the time, the flavour will have been created synthetically with chemical flavourings. Only if the yoghurt is labelled 'strawberry yoghurt' will a significant proportion come from actual strawberries. Even then, the processing business typically robs so much of the strawberry's natural flavour that in many cases it has to be at least enhanced artificially. This is so much the norm that it's a unique selling point if a strawberry yoghurt actually gets its flavour from strawberries and yoghurt, and it will be promoted as pure, fresh strawberry yoghurt to make sure you know.

Whenever you see the words 'flavour' or 'flavouring' you can be sure that the flavour of the food has been created synthetically from chemicals. A 'strawberry flavour' yoghurt has never been anywhere near a real strawberry. The word 'flavoured', however, is a bit of grey area. If a yoghurt is said to be 'strawberry flavoured', it probably means that although the flavour is essentially synthetic, real strawberries have actually been added.

The term 'natural' can be equally misleading. You might think that, if a food company advertises something as full of natural strawberry flavours, then the flavour actually comes from strawberries. This is not always true. The flavour industry has learned to analyse the chemical make-up of flavours that occur naturally, such as strawberries. Then, using a chemical tool-box, they can mimic the strawberry's flavour and make it industrially in a chemical plant. Because this chemical flavour mimics the flavour of a real fruit, the food industry may call it a natural flavour. When you see 'natural strawberry flavour' on a label, it doesn't necessarily mean that the flavour comes from strawberries; it could just mean that it contains chemicals that give it a similar taste to real strawberries. Some flavour chemists will tell you that this natural flavour is literally identical to the real thing. However, natural flavours are actually far too complex to mimic identically, so it's only an approximation. In an attempt to avoid confusion, some countries' regulations distinguish between 'natural' and 'nature identical' flavours. Natural flavours are flavourings that are at least derived from the natural product – but even these can be added to the food artificially. Nature identical flavours are flavours created entirely artificially to mimic natural flavours.

Flavours are described as artificial only if they are chemical flavours that have no counterpart in nature. Ethyvanillin, for instance, is an artificial flavour a little like the natural vanillin flavour of vanilla, but three to four times as strong. Such strong flavours are often needed to make heavily processed foods taste interesting.

36. 47% of broiler chickens sold suffer from crippling bone disorders

One of the biggest changes in food habits around the world in the last 30 years has been the phenomenal rise in eating chicken. In the past, people used to eat chicken only rarely, for celebrations such as Christmas. It was an expensive luxury. Now people eat far more chicken than any other meat.

In the UK alone, sales of chicken have gone up five-fold in the last twenty years, and brands like Kentucky Fried Chicken have made an impact all around the world. In a year, people in the UK eat a total of 820 million chickens – that's an entire chicken every two to three weeks for every man, woman and child.

The astonishing rise in chicken-eating has gone hand-in-hand with a little-noticed revolution in chicken farming. Chicken farming has become industrialised and globalised. Only a tiny proportion of the world's chickens are now brown, egg-laying hens scratching around in the open. The vast majority are now white 'broilers' reared solely for their meat in huge chicken factories. All around the world there are now enormous, dark sheds where tens of thousands of these chickens are raised from chicks, fattened and slaughtered in just a few months.

The scale of the industry is staggering. In just three American states, for instance – Georgia, Arkansas and Alabama – nearly 4 billion chickens are raised and slaughtered every year. A huge proportion of this vast industry is concentrated in the hands of just a few American global agribusinesses – Tysons, Gold Kist,

ConAgra, Pilgrim's Pride and Cargill – which control the process right through from chicken to abattoir and beyond.

The chicken produced by this factory system is abundant and incredibly cheap. A whole chicken now may cost little more than a pint of beer. But there are downsides. In the 1940s, it took 80 days or more for chickens to reach their full market weight of 2kg. Now, thanks to genetic selection and feeding techniques, they grow twice as fast. In effect, the chickens reach adult size before they have even reached puberty. This rapid growth creates a number of welfare problems for the birds.

When a chicken's body grows this fast its organs can't keep up, and so many just keel over and die from heart attacks, or 'flipovers' as some chicken farmers call them. Worse still, the chickens' bodies grow faster than their skeletons, and their leg bones become far too weak to support their bloated bodies. Surveys have found that 47% of broiler chickens sold suffer from the painful leg bone disorder dyschondroplasia. In fact, most of these chickens are completely unable to walk. And because they are unable to walk, many of them spend a long time sitting in poor quality litter, giving them severe breast blisters and hock burns.

37. The food industry spends $40 billion on advertising food every year

We don't need to be persuaded to buy food; it's a necessity of life. Yet the food industry spends $40 billion (£21 billion) a year advertising it. That's $7 for every single man, woman and child on the planet. In rich countries like the USA, the spending on food advertising isn't far short of $100 (£53) per person.

The heaviest advertising comes from American global brands like Coca-Cola, McDonald's and Pepsi. Coca-Cola spends $1.5 billion advertising every year, making it and McDonald's the two most globally recognised brands. About a quarter of this is spent in the USA, of course, but in recent years Coca-Cola and the other food giants like Nestlé, Procter & Gamble and Mars have been targeting the ex-Soviet countries with a vengeance.

Of course, the food that gets all the advertisement is rarely fresh food. It's almost invariably processed food, food with high added value. This is food we don't necessarily need, but can be persuaded to buy because it seems to suit our taste or lifestyle – fizzy drinks, sweets, fast food and so on.

The problem is that these foods are almost invariably much higher in sugars, refined starches, fats and added salt than fresh food – and they include the very junk foods that health practitioners believe are fuelling the obesity epidemic that's now sweeping the richer world and bringing many health problems such as heart disease and diabetes. In a telling comparison, Eric Millstone and Tim Lang say in their book, *The Atlas of Food*, that 'for every dollar spent by the World Health Organization on trying to improve the nutrition of the world's population, around $500 is spent by the food industry on promoting processed foods'.

In face of the rising tide of obesity and diabetes, many health experts are calling for bans to be placed on advertising junk food, especially to children, who are particularly susceptible to advertising's persuasive power and are the target of a huge proportion of junk food advertising. Some organisations believe that there should be no advertising of junk food on TV before 9pm.

So far, governments have held off from any such bans, and are trying to encourage voluntary restraint from the food industry. In the UK, the health minister Patricia Hewitt said: 'We've already stepped in, but there's only so much the government can do ... People need to want to change their lifestyles and take responsibility for their health.'

38. Cheese contains ten times the amount of the two supposed feel-good chemicals in chocolate

Any food containing carbohydrates can improve your mood. Carbohydrates, such as cereals, pasta and anything sweet, have a calming, anxiety-reducing effect because they increase production of the nerve signal-transmitting chemical serotonin in the brain. A good serotonin level makes you feel calm and relaxed. Too much makes you drowsy, which is why you often feel sleepy after a heavy lunch. All high-fat, high-sugar foods improve your mood like this. Chocolate has the added bonus of a chemical called phenylethylamine (PEA), which stimulates the nerves to release chemicals called endorphins as well as serotonin. Endorphins are natural painkillers that, like morphine, induce a sense of mild euphoria. It also contains theobromines, which are a mild, mood-enhancing stimulant, far gentler and more pleasant than caffeine. Cheese actually contains ten times as much PEA and theobromine as chocolate, which is probably why many people get cheese cravings and it has a reputation as an aphrodisiac. However, it doesn't have the serotonin-boosting sugar that chocolate does.

39. The aroma of liquorice may be a genuine aphrodisiac

For thousands of years, people have searched for a food that would stimulate romance. Oysters, avocados, chocolate, champagne, steak, spices and many more foods have been called into service by the would-be lover. High claims have been made for the aphrodisiac powers of substances, especially foods. Yet there has been little, if any, scientific evidence to back up the claims of any substance to stimulate sexual desire. A few, like Viagra, of course, and yohimbine (an extract of the bark of an African tree) may stimulate performance, but none actually boost libido.

Scientists recognise that both food and sex stimulate the same pleasure chemical, dopamine, inside the brain, so it's perhaps not surprising that we link food and sex. But there's no real proof that eating anything could make you want to have more sex. In 2006, clinical tests were under way on a substance called bremelanotide, inhaled as a nasal spray, which has been shown to increase libido. Spanish fly has long been known to inflame the genitals. And oysters have been found to contain the chemicals D aspartic acid and NMDA, which encourage the body to release the sex hormones oestrogen and testosterone. But there's little proof of any food raising libido other than psychologically.

Many animals secrete aromatic chemicals called pheromones, which act as chemical messengers to stimulate mating, but attempts to prove the effectiveness of similar chemicals in humans have so far come to little. All the same, the nose is stimulated to engorge with blood by the right smells, just as the penis and vagina are before sex, for obvious reasons. So if food does have aphrodisiac qualities, it may well work through aroma. Experimenters at Chicago's Smell and Taste Treatment and Research Foundation tested which smells provoked the strongest increase of blood flow to the genitals. They found that dough-nuts stimulated blood flow to the penis by an average of 32%, while cucumber boosted vaginal blood flow by 13%. The smell of liquorice did it for both men and women.

In 2007, Turn On Beverages are launching their cherry-tasting TURN ON Love Drink range of soft drinks, which they claim increases 'sexual energy and desire, while heightening the senses and intensifying pleasure'. This, they say, is the result of its 'potent variety of active herbs (such as ginseng), amino acids and vitamins including Schizandra, a herb native to China that has been used for centuries for its aphrodisiac effect, and Guarana, a South American forbidden love fruit reputed to be a powerful aphrodisiac'. It all sounds too good to be true, and probably is.

40. Dessert is traditionally served after dinner because of 17th-century concerns about sugar

In medieval times, sugar was widely considered good for health and assumed a prominent place in meals. But in the 17th century, physicians began to look at the body in terms of chemistry. Physicians began to view digestion as a chemical process like distillation and fermentation, and classified foods according to their chemistry. They began to advocate 'cool' salads and green vegetables to balance the natural 'hot' acidity of the stomach, and the diarist John Evelyn wrote the first popular book on salads. Sugar was considered a 'hot', acidic food. Physicians began to see the link of sugar to black teeth and the disease later called diabetes. Indeed, it began to acquire a reputation as an unhealthy food. 'Under its whiteness, sugar hides a great blackness', said the French royal physician Joseph Duchesne in 1606. Sugar, once a central part of the menu, began to be removed to the periphery, to be served as a mere afterpiece, a dessert to help the digestion. It has remained there ever since.

41. In the USA, the key tool in government advice for the general public on nutrition is the food pyramid

Back in 1992, the US Department of Agriculture came up with a simple graphic device to help remind people of the different proportions of the main food groups they should include in their diet for good health. The wide base of the pyramid showed that the bulk of your food (6–11 servings a day) should be complex carbohydrates (bread, cereal, rice and pasta) to provide energy. Above that came slightly less fruit (2–4 servings) and vegetables (3–5 servings). On top of that came protein – fish, poultry, eggs, nuts and beans (2–3 servings) and milk, yoghurt and cheese (2–3 servings). The narrow apex of the pyramid, to be eaten only sparingly, was fats, oil and sweets.

When the pyramid was being developed, the average American got about 40% of his energy from fat, 15% from protein and 45% from carbohydrates. The prime aim of the pyramid was to cut the portion of fat in the diet, because it was thought that fat was bad for you. Nutritionists decided, with no real evidence, that no more than 30% of your energy should come from fat, and this was the main point of the food pyramid. Since 1992, of course, nutritionists have come to realise that this idea isn't really valid. Scientists have discovered, for instance, that there are two kinds of cholesterol-carrying chemicals involved in heart disease (LDL, 'bad cholesterol', and HDL, 'good cholesterol'). Simply replacing saturated fats in your diet with carbohydrates reduces both LDL and HDL, so the ratio of bad cholesterol to good does not improve. Indeed, the extra carbohydrate boosts blood triglyceride levels, increasing the risk of heart disease.

So in 2005, the USDA decided to issue a revised food pyramid to reflect these discoveries. The idea was to emphasise the value of whole grains, to distinguish between types of fat and give better choices for protein. It also included a figure climbing the pyramid to promote the values of exercise. But unlike the earlier pyramid it does not give any simple-to-remember general dietary recommendations. To find out your personal recommended diet, you must visit USDA's website (www.mypyramid. gov), where you can generate your own custom-made pyramid according to your age, sex and level of daily physical activity.

42. Polytunnels give Spanish lettuce growers four crops a year

People have long been aware of how the globalisation of supermarkets' food sourcing, combined with advanced chilling techniques, has made the seasonality of food almost disappear. We can buy fresh strawberries and salads in winter, apples and peaches in spring, and most vegetables all year round – because they can either be frozen or brought in from wherever they are in season. Now the development of polytunnels has meant that many fruit and vegetables can even be grown all year round too.

Polytunnels are tunnels of clear polythene stretched in rows over the fields to completely enclose the crop and grow it in an entirely artificial environment. Polytunnels act like a greenhouse and keep the crop warm in winter, extending the growing season. They protect the crop from storm damage and also help cut evaporation, saving on water.

Using polytunnels, growers in England have been able to produce everything from lettuces and onions to strawberries and raspberries over much longer periods, and so compete with imported fruit. In places like Hereford, huge amounts of strawberries are now grown under plastic, and UK strawberry production doubled between 2002 and 2006, hitting 50,000 tonnes.

In dry areas around the Mediterranean, the impact of polytunnels has been even more dramatic. Now vast areas of the once almost desert-like region of Spain around Almería – scene of many a spaghetti western – are covered in plastic. Under these shiny tunnels, huge quantities of salad vegetables and soft fruit are grown not in soil but in bags of oven-puffed white stone perlite. The stability of climate conditions under the plastic means that up to four crops of lettuce can be grown each year. Similar scenes are visible in countries like Morocco and Algeria.

But there may be real downsides to polytunnel culture. In the UK, protesters have highlighted their visual impact, with natural farmland covered in acres of billowing plastic. Elsewhere, other problems are emerging. Polytunnel culture in semi-arid regions demands vast amounts of water. In places like Morocco, all of this water is pumped up from beneath the ground, with the result that groundwater is so depleted that peasants are often unable to farm and so are forced off the land.

The enclosed environment of the polytunnel can mean that the crops are particularly susceptible to pests too. Many critics suggest that, to combat these pests, farmers might use pesticides very heavily. Since the crops grown under plastic are typically salad vegetables and soft fruit that are particularly prone to the take-up of pesticides, there has been some concern that polytunnel salad vegetables may pose health problems, such as an increased risk of breast cancer.

43. Antibiotic-resistant GM bacteria, introduced to help make crops self-fertilising, are now widespread in American soil

One of the main problems facing modern farming is the need for huge amounts of artificial fertiliser. Farmers today need to use ten times as much nitrogen fertiliser to get good yields as they did 40 years ago. This is not only expensive, but can damage the soil and the environment.

Yet not all crops need artificial fertilisers. Legumes do not. Legumes are plants that make pods, like peas and beans. Legumes have a close relationship with bacteria called *Rhizobium meliloti*. The *Rhizobium* bacteria live on the legume's roots and form swellings called nodules. Both plant and bacteria benefit from this relationship. The bacteria get a home and food in the form of sugars made by the plant. In return, the bacteria convert nitrogen from the air into ammonia, a deal called nitrogen-fixing. Plants cannot use nitrogen in the air, but they can use it in the form of ammonia. Cereal crops need this ammonia added in the form of nitrogen fertilisers. Legumes have the bacteria to make it for them.

In the 1990s, scientists discovered why *Rhizobium* lives in legume roots and not in cereals. Legume roots produce chemicals called flavonoids which attract the bacteria; cereals also make flavonoids, but not the right ones. So scientists began to wonder if they could introduce genes for legume flavonoids into cereals. They also wondered if they could alter the genes of the bacteria so that they were attracted by different flavonoids. This line proved quickly fruitful. In 1997, scientists had altered the genes of the bacteria that normally invade peas so that they invade clover instead. Now they are working to develop bacteria that will invade cereal crops. If they can do that, the cereals will grow nitrogen-fixing nodules on their roots. They will then become self-fertilising.

In the meantime, scientists have genetically modified the *Sinorhizobium meliloti* bacteria that live on legumes. These bacteria are even more attracted to legumes and even better at fixing nitrogen than natural bacteria. GM bacteria are now in widespread use in America and have spread throughout the soil in many areas. Most soil contains fungi that create natural antibiotics, chemicals that attack bacteria. In fact, most antibiotic drugs come from soil fungi. So the bacteria that help legumes fix nitrogen could well be attacked by natural antibiotics in the soil. To stop this happening, scientists creating the GM bacteria *Sinorhizobium meliloti* also added genes that make them resistant to natural antibiotics such as streptomycin. The concern is that if antibiotic-resistant bacteria are spread in the soil, antibiotic resistance will become so widespread among bacteria that antibiotic drugs lose their power to fight disease.

44. 60% of deaths around the world are related to changes in diet and increased consumption of fatty, salty and sugary food

In 2003, the World Health Organization issued a massive and groundbreaking annual report. It summarised one of the largest research projects ever undertaken into the health of the world. The idea was to identify which factors posed the greatest risks to the health of the world's population in the years to come and what could be done to ameliorate the risks. The report identified the ten leading risk factors globally as: underweight; unsafe sex; high blood pressure; tobacco consumption; alcohol consumption; unsafe water, sanitation and hygiene; iron deficiency; indoor smoke from solid fuels; high cholesterol; and obesity.

What became overwhelmingly clear was that most of the risks are related to patterns of living and consumption – people's health is at risk if they consume too little or too much. For people in the developed world, the message was loud and clear. Diet is indisputably linked with health, and the association of particular eating patterns with cancer and cardiovascular disease is clear. After tobacco, diet is the greatest single preventable cause of ill health.

The report found that 60% of world deaths are 'clearly related to changes in dietary patterns and increased consumption of processed fatty, salty and sugary foods'. It said blood pressure causes more deaths worldwide than tobacco (7m compared with 5m), and in the industrialised countries of North America, Europe and Asia, at least a third of all disease is caused by tobacco, alcohol, high blood pressure, cholesterol and obesity.

Obesity is the real heavyweight problem. People are not just eating far more than they need in sheer quantity, but they have packed their plates with energy-rich high-fat, high-sugar foods which are simply laid down as fat when combined with an inactive lifestyle. The result is that the average weight is rising by the minute. According to *The Guardian*: 'In Britain in 1974, only 7% of children were obese. Now 22% are. So are 21% of British men, and 23% of women. At a conservative estimate it costs the NHS £3bn a year in treatment and lost working days. In America, where health costs are higher, the figure is a whopping $123bn. There, the obesity rate is 30%, rising to 40% among Mexican Americans and 50% of black American women. Of those 50%, 15% have extreme obesity, or are morbidly obese and it gets worse. There are islands in the Pacific where 80% of the adult population is obese.'

Obesity has a crucial adverse impact on health, including increases in blood pressure, unfavourable cholesterol levels and increased resistance to insulin. Each dramatically raises the risks of coronary heart disease, stroke, diabetes mellitus, and many forms of cancer. The WHO report showed that obesity was killing about 220,000 men and women a year in the USA and Canada alone, and about 320,000 men and women in 20 countries of Western Europe. And if you survive into old age, the extra toll of weight on your joints increases your chances of osteoarthritis ...

45. The average fourteen-year-old today is taller than the average soldier in the Boer War 100 years ago because of improved nutrition

Although the abundance of food available to people in the Western world has begun to create its own health problems, there is no doubt that good nutrition has allowed children today to reach their full physical potential in a way that would have been impossible for the average child a century ago. People today are, on average, 10cm taller than they were at the time of the Boer War.

There are, of course, many reasons why we are taller today, including the reduction of disease, but the big contributor is certainly better food. Back in the time of the Boer War, all but the few better-off subsisted largely on a diet of heavy carbohydrates – bread, potato and so on. Good protein foods like milk and meat were a rare treat. Without a decent supply of proteins, children's growth was stunted. Only with the increasing availability of cheap protein in the 20th century did children begin to grow tall. Throughout the last century, people gained a centimetre in height on average in every decade.

Conventional wisdom has it that average height has steadily increased through the ages, and that we're now taller than ever before. But Professor Richard Steckel of Ohio University has studied the height of thousands of male skeletons buried in northern Europe dating right back to the 9th century, and turned this idea on its head. What is interesting is that between the 9th and 11th centuries, men were, on average, almost as tall as they are today

– and they were considerably taller than they were on the eve of the Industrial Revolution. After reaching well over 173cm on average at the end of the Middle Ages, men shrank to an all-time low of 167cm in the 18th century, and didn't begin to grow tall again until the 20th century.

Steckel offers a variety of explanations for this long dip in height, including climate change and urbanisation. A cooling of the climate from the Middle Ages on, leading to what is sometimes known as the Little Ice Age (when ice fairs were held on the Thames), may have shortened crop-growing seasons and deprived people of food. The rapid growth of cities in the Industrial Revolution may also have denied people access to good, fresh food, while promoting the spread of disease.

Of course, throughout this period, the rich always had access to good food and good conditions, and so remained tall. Only the poor had their growth stunted by lack of food. The same is true on a global scale today.

46. Milk from cloned, genetically modified farm animals could be medicines for the future

Genetically modified crops have been with us since the mid-1970s, but farm animals have proved much harder to engineer. The problem was that any engineered change could not be replicated. In 1997, for instance, scientists created Rosie, the world's first GM dairy cow, along with eight other similarly modified cows. Rosie was engineered to produce a human protein called alpha-lactalbumin in her milk. Alpha-lactalbumin is found in human milk, and most babies get it through breast-feeding, but babies who are born prematurely cannot breast-feed. Rosie's milk could be fed to them in powdered form. The problem is that these modified cows were one-offs, so the modifications could not be passed on. The answer, scientists realised, is to clone animals – that is, create living copies that are genetically identical. The famous breakthrough, of course, came in the mid-1990s when the Roslin Institute in Edinburgh created Dolly the sheep, the world's first cloned farm animal. Although Dolly was a clone, her genes were unmodified. So in 1998, the biotech company PPL worked with the Roslin scientists to produce another sheep, which they called Polly. Like Dolly, Polly was a clone. The difference was that Polly's genes were modified. Her genes included a human gene that would enable Polly to produce a protein in her milk that made blood clot. This protein, called Factor IX, could be used to help treat people with the disease haemophilia. Such cloned GM animals are still in the experimental stage. (See also Fact 54.)

47. It takes more than three hours to burn off the energy in a small packet of crisps

In our distant past, energy-rich foods such as sugars and fats were hard to come by. So our bodies have evolved to lap them up when they become available. But for most people in developed countries, such foods are now abundant – so abundant that they are beginning to make us overweight and at risk of illnesses like heart disease. The problem is that any energy food we eat that is not burned off may turn to fat.

Our bodies do need energy to keep ticking over, even if we are doing absolutely nothing – to keep the heart beating and the lungs breathing and to keep warm, for instance. This is known as resting metabolism. Resting Metabolic Rate or RMR varies considerably from person to person, and from time to time, according to age and environmental conditions. But the amount of energy burned in resting metabolism is never very big.

The average person burns about 60 joules of energy every second just sitting doing nothing. That's about the same as a 60 watt light bulb. It might sound like quite a lot, but there's a lot of energy in sugary and fatty food. In fact, just a couple of crisps contain as much energy as a large cabbage. As the packet will tell you, there's maybe 172 calories in a small packet of crisps. That's 724 kilojoules, or 724,000 joules of energy packed into that tiny bag. So that little bag of crisps will take you 12,000 seconds – or three hours twenty minutes – to burn off.

Only when you get up and begin to exercise do you really begin to burn off energy. Energy consumption soars when you're really working out. Even so, you'd have to run hard for almost half an hour to burn off the energy in just two small packets of crisps. One good thing about exercise, though, is that it raises the rate at which you burn energy not just while you're hard at it, but for a couple of hours afterwards.

If you take in more energy than your body burns, your body saves it for times of shortage – that is, it converts it to fat. If you eat 3,500 calories more than you burn, you'll gain a pound in fat. Eat just two small packets of crisps a day above what your body needs in terms of energy, and you'll put on a pound (0.45kg) in little more than a week and nearly a stone (6.35kg) in three months. Conversely, if you take in less energy food than your body needs, you lose fat – at pretty much the same rate. It's a simple equation.

Some things increase your RMR, such as extra muscle, living in a cold place and eating small, regular meals. So can being pregnant. Some things decrease it, such as getting older and crash dieting (because you lose muscle, not just fat) – which is why it's so easy to regain weight after going on a crash diet.

48. 'McDonald's food contains so many preservatives and chemicals that it doesn't grow mould'

This is not a fact, but an assertion by Morgan Spurlock, creator of the famous anti-fast-food film *Super Size Me*. Spurlock describes how he conducted a number of trials with McDonald's food and found no signs of mould growing on his Mac french fries even after many months. He quotes the example, too, of a man who has a whole collection of apparently indestructible McDonald's foods dating from the early 1990s.

There is of course no scientific proof of these assertions, nor is it clear what the implications are if it's true. Nevertheless, it focuses attention on the issue of the levels of preservatives in food.

Foods go off mainly because microbes such as bacteria and fungi grow on them, or because they are affected by oxygen, in a process called oxidation. Oxidation is what makes an apple go brown when you slice it and expose the surface to the air. Foods can be salted or pickled, and smoked, dried, frozen or canned to stop them going off, or they can be treated with chemical preservatives. There are now 30 or so of these chemical preservatives that may be legally added to food. They work either against microbes, or against oxidation, or both. Benzoates are added to fruit juices, margarine, jams, pickles and many other foods to extend their shelf-life by stopping fungal growth. Sulphur dioxide and other sulphites are coated onto dried fruit and vegetables to stop them going brown and to stop bacteria growing. Propionates are added to bread to stop it going mouldy.

There's no doubt that preservatives have made food available and edible for longer. They can even be life-savers. Nitrates and nitrites are the food industry's best defence against the botulin bacteria in meat, as well as helping to preserve the meat's pink colour. And in 2006, it was discovered that nitrite food preservatives might one day be used to help treat patients with the lung disease cystic fibrosis.

But doubts have been raised about the effects of some preservatives on the human body. Some are clearly linked to specific allergic reactions, for instance. Sulphites trigger asthma attacks in allergic people by making airways tight. So sulphite-sensitive asthmatics are advised to avoid food containing sulphite preservatives with the E numbers 221–228. Foods served in restaurants, such as french fries, often contain sulphites. So does bottled lemon juice. Benzoates can sometimes have similar effects, and those who might be allergic are warned against the E numbers 210–215 and 217. Other research also links food preservatives to hyperactivity in children.

It has long been an urban myth that corpses today don't decay as fast as they did in the past because of the amount of food preservatives that have built up in our bodies. After watching the decay of exhumed human remains buried over the last 30 years, Professor Rainer Horn of Kiel University in Germany has concluded that this is actually true. He believes that the combination of food preservatives and cosmetics is literally embalming us while we are still alive.

49. Junk food can impair mental ability

When it comes to energy, the brain is the most demanding organ in the body. Although the brain is just 2% or less of your body weight, it uses a fifth of the body's energy intake. This is why eating enough energy food is crucial for good brain function. Energy in food comes in the form of chemicals called carbohydrates, such as sugars and starches. The brain can use them only in one form, glucose, so the body has to convert most carbohydrates into glucose for the brain to benefit. The glucose is delivered to the brain in the blood.

Some sweet foods, such as fizzy drinks, sweets and many fast foods, contain sugars in simple forms that are very easily absorbed and quickly changed into glucose. You might think that this would be great for the brain, providing instant energy. Unfortunately, it's just too useable. Just as paper is great for getting a fire started but burns too quickly to sustain a steady blaze, so sugary foods are just too readily burned up to make good brain food if consumed in large quantities.

Sugary foods are so easily converted by the body into glucose that there's a sudden rise in blood sugar levels. The body quickly produces insulin in response to this sugar rush, in an effort to bring the levels down. The result is that blood sugar levels swing wildly from high to low.

In the short term, this can cause dizziness, anxiety, headaches, thirst, confusion and tiredness. In the long term, a diet with excess sugars can slow down the activity of the brain as it adjusts to these continuous floods of blood sugar. Feed the body continually with a high-sugar diet and it adjusts by becoming less sensitive to insulin. Low insulin sensitivity means that body cells, especially brain cells, begin to starve themselves of sugar. Toronto Professor Carol Greenwood showed that people with insulin resistance, who were already slower learners, got much worse after a sugary snack.

Studies by California neurosurgeon Fernando Gomez-Pinilla of mice fed on what are effectively junk food diets, known by neuroscientists as HFS (high-fat, high-sugar diets), show a marked decline in the ability to perform tasks of mental agility, and in the ability to recover from mild head injuries. Gomez-Pinilla showed that mice on the HFS diet also had reduced levels of a chemical protein called brain-derived neurotrophic factor (BDNF). BDNF is thought to be important in encouraging neurons to grow and make new connections.

Gomez-Pinilla also believes that the high calorie levels in an HFS diet help to generate free radicals. Free radicals play a key role in the ageing process by damaging cell membranes, proteins and DNA, the cell's master chemicals. Neurons are thought to be especially susceptible to free radical damage. It seems that the more high-octane fuel you feed your brain, the faster it burns out – and the worse it performs.

50. It takes 2–3kg of fishmeal protein to produce each kilogram of farmed fish protein

In the last twenty years, the amount of fish produced on farms has soared, doubling between 1985 and 2000 and now providing well over a quarter of all the world's fish. Over 220 different species of fish are now grown in cages, tanks, ponds and lagoons around the world.

People sometimes think of fish farming as being good for the environment because it takes some of the huge pressure on the world's wild fish. This is certainly true of some farmed fish. Carp raised in flooded paddy fields in China, for instance, feed on plant debris, and so add to the world's fish stocks and reduce demand for wild fish. It's not true, however, of the more than 700 million tonnes of Atlantic salmon farmed annually. Salmon are carnivores, so they cannot be fed on plant matter. Instead, they are fed on fishmeal prepared from ocean-caught fish such as mackerel. It takes 2–3kg of fishmeal protein to produce each kilogram of farmed fish protein. So salmon fish farms actually increase the pressure on wild fish stocks.

51. A strawberry milk-shake in a fast-food outlet contains at least 59 ingredients; making one at home takes four

In his book *Chew on This*, a children's follow-up to his famous exposé of the fast-food industry, *Fast Food Nation*, Eric Schlosser compares the number of ingredients in a strawberry milk-shake from a fast-food outlet with one made at home. The idea is to highlight just what elaborate chemical concoctions processed foods have become – concoctions that bear scant resemblance to the natural originals.

A home-made strawberry milk-shake, Schlosser points out, can be made from just four simple ingredients – milk, strawberries, sugar and just a touch of vanilla. In fast-food strawberry milk-shake, however, you might find: milk-fat and non-fat milk, sugar, sweet whey, high-fructose corn syrup, guar gum, monoglycerides and diglycerides, cellulose gum, sodium phosphate, carrageenan, citric acid, E129 and artificial strawberry flavour. That phrase 'artificial strawberry flavour', Schlosser emphasises, involves a long list of chemicals mixed to give the appropriate taste: amyl acetate, amyl butyrate, amyl valerate, anethol, anisyl formate, benzyl acetate, benzyl isobutyrate, butyric acid, cinnamyl isobutyrate, cinnamyl valerate, cognac essential oil, diacetyl, dipropyl ketone, ethyl butyrate, ethyl cinnamate, ethyl heptanoate, ethyl heptylate, ethyl lactate, ethyl methylphenylglycidate, ethyl nitrate, ethyl propionate, ethyl valerate, heliotropin, hydroxyphrenyl-2-butanone (10% solution in alcohol), ionone, isobutyl anthranilate, isobutyl butyrate, lemon essential oil, maltol,

4-methylacetophenone, methyl anthranilate, methyl benzoate, methyl cinnamate, methyl heptine carbonate, methyl naphthyl ketone, methyl salicylate, mint essential oil, neroli essential oil, nerolin, neryl isobutyrate, orris butter, phenethyl alcohol, rose, rum ether, undecalactone, vanillin and solvent.

Of course, the comparison is somewhat pejorative, as critics of Schlosser point out, since any flavour, natural or otherwise, is a combination of the aromas of scores, if not hundreds, of different chemicals. Schlosser's point, though, is firstly just how divorced from natural flavours fast food has become, and secondly how the process is playing on children's tendency to avoid bitter tastes. Natural fruits combine sweetness and bitterness to give their distinctive taste. When flavourists create artificial strawberry for children, they get rid of the bitterness to create a sweet bubblegum kind of flavour. Children therefore may become used to sweet tastes and sweet food, and steer clear of anything with a trace of bitterness. No wonder, then, that children – and the adults they grow into – are drawn to consume an excess of sugary foods.

52. Instant coffee, typically costing $25 or more per kilo, may be bought from growers at just 14 cents per kilo, a mark-up of 7,000%

Coffee is a huge industry worth hundreds of billions of pounds. Around the world, there are some 25 million farmers involved in growing it, and countless more depend upon it for their livelihood. Indeed, it's hard to overestimate its importance in the economic fortunes of many Third World countries. In Africa, Ethiopia earns over half its export revenue from coffee, Burundi earns almost 80% from coffee and in Uganda a third of the population rely on coffee for their income. Central American countries such as Honduras, Costa Rica and Nicaragua are almost as dependent.

But there's a problem. Despite the massive demand for coffee in the West, the world grows too much of it, and has been since the year 2000. That was the year that Vietnam, after a massive investment in coffee-growing encouraged by the World Bank and the IMF, came from almost nowhere to become the world's second-largest coffee producer after Brazil (see Fact 8). It signalled the beginning of a glut of coffee on the world market that has led to a dramatic slump in price. In 1994, Uganda's coffee crop earned it $433 million. In 2001, it earned just $110 million, even though it was growing more coffee.

This crisis in world coffee prices is something the average coffee-drinker in the West is usually unaware of, sipping their expensive lattes and mochachinos in yet another new chain coffee outlet. The reason is added value. For the food industry, the key to making big profits is 'added value'. Foodsellers can make only so much profit on raw, unprocessed food. But processing food adds value and opens the way to big profits. When it comes to added value, instant coffee is a real winner.

Moreover, much of the global coffee industry is concentrated in a few giant corporate hands. Nestlé alone buys 13% of the world's coffee crop, and sells 57% of its instant coffee. Philip Morris–Kraft (now known as Altria) is almost as big. These two coffee giants, along with Sara Lee and Procter & Gamble, buy almost half the world's coffee.

Such concentrated buying power, such a glut of coffee, and such massive potential added value has shifted the money made from coffee dramatically away from the growers to the big multinationals. In a report aptly entitled *Mugged*, Oxfam traced the prices paid for a kilo of coffee grown in Uganda in 2002. The farmer was paid 14 US cents. The local miller took an extra 5 cents, while transport and other costs meant that the exporter bought it for 26 cents. The exporter graded and packaged it and sold it on for 45 cents. By the time it reached the big multinational who would roast the coffee and turn it into instant coffee granules, the price was $1.64. But that same kilo of coffee would sell in shops in instant form at an astonishing $26.40 – that is, 7,000% more than the farmer got for it.

53. British people buy 1.8 billion sandwiches a year

People often refer to it as the 'humble' sandwich, but consumption is anything but humble. In the UK alone, people eat 1.8 billion sandwiches every year – that's enough bread to stretch twelve times around the world. Britain is the centre of the sandwich feast, but it's replicated in other countries, such as Australia, where people eat 450 million of them a year.

The sandwich was named after the 18th-century Earl of Sandwich, who is said to have shoved ham between two slices of toast so that he could carry on gambling while eating. But it was probably invented much, much earlier. Traditionally, a sandwich is a filling between two slices of bread, but now it comes in all shapes and sizes. Wraps, toasted paninis, bagels and clubs are among the numerous varieties on offer.

Twenty years ago, the sandwich seemed old-fashioned as a snack, destined to be replaced by more exotic items such as burgers and pizzas. Yet in the last decade it has undergone an explosive renaissance. In 1996, the UK sandwich market was worth just £1.9 billion. By 2001, it had increased 47% to £2.8 billion. Just four years later, a staggering £3.5 billion worth of sandwiches were being sold in Britain each year.

Various reasons have been offered for the rise of the sandwich, but the most convincing is the change in working patterns. The days of the leisurely lunch hour are now long gone, and 86% of people take less than half an hour for lunch. 23% of people don't even leave their desks at lunch, grabbing a snack on the way to work to keep them going through the day. Interestingly, over a third of all sandwiches are sold outside the traditional lunchtime – before 10am and after 4pm. Just like the Earl of Sandwich, the modern office worker has discovered that the sandwich is the perfect snack food to keep you fed while on the go.

Keeping up with this voracious demand has become a huge business. Very rarely are sandwiches made fresh. Instead, they are made in vast sandwich factories, packed, chilled, transported over often huge distances, then stored, with inevitable consequences for taste.

About a quarter of UK sandwiches are sold through multiple retailers such as Boots, Sainsbury's and M&S. The rest are sold in workplace canteens, sandwich bars and coffee shops such as Subway and Pret à Manger, which sells £77 million worth of sandwiches every year. The sandwich king of the UK, though, is the little known Greencore, which has a 9% slice of the market, with sandwiches made at its giant factories in Manton Wood, Nottingham (3 million sandwiches a week), Park Royal, London (1 million) and Bow, London (550,000), then distributed all over the UK.

54. Trials are under way with crops genetically engineered to deliver edible vaccines

At the moment, most medicines are made in giant chemical factories. In the future, though, GM technology may mean that pharmaceuticals can be grown on farms, an idea punningly called 'pharming'.

The idea is that all kinds of animals and plants could be modified to make medicines. Sheep, goats and cows have already been modified to give medicines in their milk. Other animals could be engineered to grow organs for transplants. Animals used for meat could be altered so that their meat contained important substances such as vitamins, or substances that reduce the harmful effects of animal fats.

GM scientists are now trying to modify food plants to give edible vaccines. Normal vaccines are expensive to make and store, since they need to be refrigerated, and they need trained doctors to give them. So in poorer parts of the world, many people die from lack of proper vaccination. In 1995, an American biotech scientist called Charles Arntzen of Arizona State University wondered if the problem could be solved by putting vaccine genes in food plants. If this could be done, vaccines could be grown locally in the quantity required. Anyone eating the food from these plants would be vaccinated against the disease. The idea has been taken up widely by the biotech companies and vaccines against diarrhoea, which is a major killer in the Third World, are a key target.

But critics fear that drug-laced pharm crops could find their way into the food of unsuspecting people, with unknown consequences. It's highly unlikely that pollen from pharm crops can ever be prevented from contaminating unmodified crops. GM crops might be modified to be sterile, but many people argue that the only foolproof way to prevent accidents is to avoid modifying food crops altogether.

Back in 2002, pharmaceutical proteins left over from a pharming experiment by the Prodigene company were found growing in fields of ordinary soya beans in Iowa and Nebraska. Following this, the US government began to look at tightening up its laws on the production of pharmaceuticals in genetically modified plants. Biotech companies like Monsanto are doing their best to convince doubters of the safety of their approach.

Arntzen believes it would be a shame if such fears prevented the development of edible vaccines which could save millions of lives in the Third World. So he's continuing his experiments with them, but with a strong emphasis on safeguards. His team works in completely sealed conditions with sterile plants. And the plant he's working with is a white tomato which tastes like sawdust and cannot possibly be mistaken for food.

55. 90% of American milk comes from a single breed of cow

Throughout the developed world, the dairy industry has become dominated by one remarkable breed of cow, the Holstein-Friesian. Almost two-thirds of dairy cows in Europe, and 90% of dairy cows in North America, are Holsteins. Other breeds are still reared in places, such as the Jersey, the Normande, the Ayrshire and the Guernsey, but over the last few decades more and more dairy farmers have turned to the Holstein.

The Holstein is the most efficient milk machine ever created, turning relatively small amounts of feed into huge volumes of milk and butterfat. This has long been known, but recent advances in artificial insemination techniques in mass breeding programmes have produced huge numbers of these cows around the world.

But there are concerns that this concentration on a single breed makes the dairy industry very vulnerable. If, for instance, the Holstein were to fall victim to a new mutation of a parasite, virus or bacteria, the effects could be disastrous. With so few other cows to fall back on, the world could suddenly find itself almost without milk and butter. Livestock breeders have been very successful at breeding cows to produce huge quantities of milk, but they have never attempted to breed in disease resistance.

The Holstein could be vulnerable to global warming, too. Holsteins are very sensitive to heat, and in the hotter countries where they are raised, farmers already use expensive sprinkler systems, fans and cooling ponds to keep them cool. Any rise in global temperatures could see Holsteins wilting around the world, and there are far too few other breeds to take up the slack.

This concentration on a single breed in the dairy industry has been mirrored right across the farming world, and is raising worries. Over the last century, more than 90% of crop varieties have disappeared. In China, more than 90% of wheat varieties have been lost in the last half-century. Over the past fifteen years, 300 out of the 6,000 farm animal breeds identified by the Food and Agriculture Organization have become extinct, and two breeds are now being lost forever each week.

Such a concentration on so few strains and breeds has undoubtedly brought huge benefits in terms of production, but this not only brings with it a frightening vulnerability to catastrophic failure, but also a massive loss of choice and variety. Half a century ago, milk could be from Jersey, Guernsey or any one of a huge range of different breeds of cow, each with its own distinctive flavour. Now milk is essentially milk, which means Holstein milk.

56. About 1 in 4 people in the Western world are said to be allergic to monosodium glutamate

Glutamate is a common amino acid found naturally in human bodies, where it's essential for cell repair, and in many different food substances. In fact, most protein-rich foods contain glutamate, including human breast milk, in what is called 'bound' form, because it's linked to other amino acids. Glutamate is also the substance that in 'free' form gives the great savoury 'umami' taste to foods like tomatoes, mushrooms, yeast, strong cheese and soya sauce (see Fact 5). In Asian cuisine, it was the reason why for centuries seaweed was added to food to boost flavour. In 1907, Japanese scientist Kikunae Ikeda in Tokyo found the key flavour ingredient in seaweed was glutamate. Ikeda then found a way to mass-produce this flavour ingredient as a white powder, a sodium salt of glutamate called monosodium glutamate or MSG. Ikeda made MSG from seaweed, but now it's made by the fermentation of corn starch, sugar cane or beet.

MSG was closely identified with food in Chinese restaurants, but it has come to be an ingredient in all kinds of processed foods, including soups, stock cubes, frozen dinners, instant meals and crisps. It's added to make up for the flavours lost in processing, or to allow less of the real thing to be used. The use of MSG is growing year by year, and over 1.5 million tonnes are used in food annually.

In the 1970s, Doctor John Olney discovered that high levels of MSG in food caused brain damage in infant mice. Public pressure soon forced baby-food companies to stop adding MSG to their products, added only in order to make them taste better to parents. Later, MSG was linked to an allergic reaction with symptoms including thirst, nausea, dizziness, sweats and headaches that came to be known as 'Chinese Restaurant Syndrome'. Ever since, a debate has continued about the health implications of MSG. According to Dr Michael Sharon: 'It is estimated that some 25% of the Western population is allergic to MSG, in one way or another.' When MSG is added to food, it must be listed as an ingredient in America, Europe and Australia – although it may be described as 'modified food starch', 'autolysed food yeast' and 'glutamic acid' rather than MSG.

However, the European Union classify MSG as completely safe – as safe as salt and baking powder. So too do the UN Food and Agriculture Organization and the World Health Organization. Various scientific studies have concluded that it's not an allergen, and that Chinese Restaurant Syndrome is a myth.

57. Wal-Mart is the world's largest retailer, with annual sales of well over $250 billion

The sheer scale of the US grocer and general merchandise giant Wal-Mart is hard to imagine. It's not just the world's biggest retailer by a long, long way: it's one of the world's two biggest global corporations, rivalled only by Exxon-Mobil. Even businesses like General Motors and General Electric are small in comparison. In the USA, it sells more groceries than all the next half dozen major chains put together – and the pattern is repeated across the world. In August 2006, Wal-Mart was doing pretty much a billion dollars of business every single day.

Wal-Mart has one overriding strategy – bringing goods to its customers at the lowest possible price. There's no doubt that this strategy has been phenomenally successful. Wal-Mart can sell food cheaper than any of its rivals. It benefits by undercutting them and seeing them all off. Customers benefit from amazing value for money, and access to food cheaper than ever before.

But Wal-Mart's dominance of sales gives it unprecedented power over its suppliers. For many suppliers, maintaining sales to Wal-Mart has become literally make or break. If a supplier loses a Wal-Mart contract, it might have to boost sales to other outlets by ten-fold or more – at the same time that Wal-Mart's upward drive is forcing more and more of these outlets out of business.

Wal-Mart's relationship with its suppliers is intense. Many would describe it as tough but fair. It's certainly tough. It demands a ruthless level of efficiency from suppliers – and drives their output towards the lowest possible prices.

A successful contract with Wal-Mart means ready access for suppliers to a massive market. But soaring sales may come at a cost. In 1999, American premium dill pickle supplier Vlacic became locked into supplying giant gallon jars of pickles for less than $3. These amazing value jumbo-sized jars sold in vast numbers – so vast that much of the US pickle crop went into them. It didn't seem to matter that most customers couldn't get through more than a quarter of the jar before it went mouldy. But for Vlacic, although sales were massive, profits were diminishingly small. By 2001, Vlacic was bankrupt.

To live with Wal-Mart's low cost drive, suppliers have to cut their costs and profits to a minimum. Sometimes this means a brutal streamlining of operations. Sometimes it means that they concentrate on cost-cutting at the expense of all else. Many suppliers to Wal-Mart have achieved the necessary cost reductions only by outsourcing to low-wage countries like China. Even household brands are affected. Jeans icon Levi-Strauss has gone entirely from being a high-class American clothes-maker to an importer of cheap Third World jeans within just two years of embarking on a contract with Wal-Mart. Food suppliers are moving the same way.

58. Honey may contain significant levels of antibiotics

Honey has an image as a natural, pure, unprocessed food. That's largely true, but recently beekeepers around the world have been using antibiotics heavily to protect their bees from diseases such as European foul brood. Foul brood disease is so devastating – wiping out whole colonies – that the temptation for beekeepers to use antibiotics is all too obvious. The problem is that residues of the antibiotics inevitably find their way into the honey. Worried that people might be unwittingly consuming antibiotics by eating honey, the EU now bans many for use in beekeeping. That doesn't stop them being used in non-EU countries, however. Between 2002 and 2004, the European Union banned imports of honey from China, one of the world's largest honey producers, because it contained chloramphenicol. Using chloramphenicol for food-producing animals is illegal in the EU because in rare cases it can cause aplastic anaemia. The ban on Chinese honey was lifted in 2004, but it seems likely that antibiotics are used for bees around the world. A survey by the Consumers' Association in 2006 found traces of the antibiotic tylosin in many samples of imported honey bought in the UK. Tylosin is licensed in the EU for treating livestock, but not bees. These residues may not do you any harm, but they shouldn't be there.

59. Eating potatoes will raise your blood sugar levels more than eating an equivalent amount of castor sugar

Sugary foods that offer nothing but calories are often considered bad for you because they have no nutritional value. They are absorbed and converted into glucose so quickly that they produce sugar peaks and troughs that can be damaging to health. A rapid rise in blood sugar stimulates the release of floods of insulin, to mop up all the glucose. Widely swinging blood glucose levels may increase the risk of heart disease, while the sudden drop in glucose after insulin gets to work may make you hungry and so lead to overeating and obesity.

Nutritionists often advise eating complex carbohydrates rather than simple sugars to reduce this problem. But refined carbohydrates such as white bread and white rice can be absorbed by the body and converted into glucose almost as quickly as pure sugar. Only whole grains are absorbed slowly and steadily. Similarly, eating potatoes actually raises blood sugar levels more than castor sugar. This is because potatoes are mostly starch, which can be rapidly metabolised in the body to glucose, while castor sugar is a combination of glucose and fructose. Fructose actually takes longer to convert to glucose than starch.

60. Children in Europe and the USA eat more than twice the recommended amount of salt in their diet every day

Common salt, sodium chloride, is a key ingredient of the human body. Bodies need the sodium in salt to maintain the fluid content of the blood. They also need it to transport nutrients into body cells and to help transmit nerve impulses. Indeed, losing too much salt in sweat, faeces and urine can lead to life-threatening dehydration – which is why the body has developed complex mechanisms for keeping salt levels balanced.

Unfortunately, the body's salt-balance mechanisms were developed in response to scarce salt conditions. Nowadays, however, salt is all too common, and many of us may be consuming too much salt for the body to cope with. Very few people now sprinkle much salt on their food at the table. Instead, we get at least 75% of our salt unwittingly from processed foods, including bread. Salt is added to processed foods to help preserve it and to restore the taste often lost during processing (see also Fact 34). Extra sodium also comes in the form of monosodium glutamate.

The problem with too much salt is that it means the body retains too much fluid, perhaps increasing blood pressure. Since high blood pressure is strongly linked to strokes and heart attacks, many research scientists believe that excess salt in the diet is bad news for the heart. The expert consensus is that we should consume no more than 6g of salt a day, yet the average consumption is 9–10g. The problem is that, since most of this comes in processed food, we are completely unaware of what we are taking in. Government organisations have therefore drawn up targets for manufacturers to reduce the salt content in processed food, but there's a long way to go.

In 2006, a number of experts began to draw attention to the problem of salt in children's diets. Children need less salt, and research shows that our children may be consuming more than twice the salt they should have every day by eating processed foods such as breakfast cereals, crisps, ready meals, biscuits and pizzas, and tinned products like beans and spaghetti hoops. Professor Graham MacGregor of CASH, a group of doctors campaigning against dietary salt, says that high-salt foods are 'literally poisoning our children's futures'. He believes that a high-salt diet in childhood could lead to a range of health problems in later life, including high blood pressure, osteoporosis, kidney stones, respiratory illness and stomach cancer.

61. Bananas contain a chemical called tryptophan which makes them the perfect night-time food

Healthy, energy-packed and conveniently wrapped, bananas are one of nature's ideal fast foods. These remarkable yellow snacks are by far the most widely consumed of all fruit, and they rank only after the basic staples of rice, wheat and maize in terms of consumption. Bananas are the most profitable of all goods for UK supermarkets, and third in terms of sales after the Lottery and petrol.

Bananas are the number one energy-food among athletes. They contain three natural sugars – sucrose, fructose and glucose – combined with fibre. This combination provides an instant energy boost that is not only much less damaging than pure glucose but is sustained over quite a long time. Indeed, some studies suggest that just two bananas provide the energy for a strenuous 90-minute workout. No wonder, then, that many sports competitors, especially tennis players, eat a banana or two just before a big game.

But bananas have a number of other health benefits, too. They are good for stomach upsets, and several studies have suggested that green bananas help to repair stomach ulcers. Bananas are also very high in potassium, which makes them good for blood pressure. In fact, the US Food and Drug Administration now allows the banana industry to advertise the banana's ability to reduce the chances of a stroke. The potassium is also said to be the reason behind the banana's apparent ability to enhance mental performance, as shown by tests at a London school.

Most intriguingly, bananas help put you in a good mood because they contain a chemical called tryptophan, a protein that the body converts into another chemical called serotonin. Serotonin is a neurotransmitter, one of the chemicals that transmits signals between nerve cells. It's sometimes said to be the brain's 'reward' chemical – the one that makes you feel good when you eat well or when you're in a good mood. By adding tryptophan and boosting serotonin levels, the banana helps you feel happier and more relaxed. So even though it gives you an energy boost, a banana is the perfect bed-time snack, helping you wind down ready for sleep.

Bananas may not be with us forever, though. They are actually sterile mutants of inedible plants – in other words, they cannot be grown from seed – and so all the banana plants in the world have been created by grafting from just a few single stocks. In the 1950s, the dominant Gros Michel banana was wiped out by Panama disease, caused by a soil fungus. Now its successor, the Cavendish, is threatened by another fungal disease, black Sigatoka. Nearly all varieties of banana are susceptible to Panama or Sigatoka. Stone Age farmers in New Guinea are thought to have cultivated the banana by replanting cuttings from their stems, but if all the banana plant stock is affected, there will be no cuttings to grow bananas again.

62. 1 in 30 or so adults and 1 in 15 children suffers from an allergy or physical intolerance to a particular food

For reasons no one is certain of, food allergies have been diagnosed more and more in recent times in America and Europe. It's thought that up to 12 million Americans, and even more Europeans, suffer food allergies. A few experts argue that up to 1 in 3 people may have at least a minor food allergy.

The most common food allergies are the so-called 'Big Eight': peanuts, milk, eggs, treenuts, fish, shellfish, soyabeans and milk, together accounting for 90% of allergic reactions. Peanut, milk and egg allergies are the most common food allergies in children.

A substance someone is allergic to, called an allergen, provokes a reaction because the body's immune system identifies the allergen as a harmful substance and launches a defence against it. It releases a flood of antibodies and other defences to repel the invader, and it's these which create the symptoms of the allergy.

When food allergens enter the body, it reacts by releasing large amounts of histamine and other chemicals. A histamine 'explosion' triggers itching, sneezing, running nose, wheezing, rashes and even diarrhoea.

Sometimes the symptoms are so minor, the sufferer barely notices them or associates them with the food. Sometimes they can be much more serious, or even fatal. Very occasionally, a food allergy can be so severe that it leads to an anaphylactic shock – when the body reacts with a dramatic drop in blood pressure and a loss of consciousness.

With some allergies the reaction to the allergen is so immediate and marked that it's easy to identify. More often, though, it takes people years to realise they are allergic to a particular food. When an allergy is suspected, allergists can conduct skin tests or blood tests. Skin tests typically involve pricking the skin with a tiny amount of the allergen to see if the skin reacts by forming a red hive spot. They cannot show what happens if the person eats the allergen, but can give a quick confirmation of a suspected allergy. Blood tests yield more detailed results, including predicting the likelihood and severity of a reaction. They also allow hundreds of potential allergens to be screened in a single sample.

There is as yet no real cure for food allergies and the only treatment is to avoid the culprit food. In future, some scientists hope to create genetically engineered vaccines.

63. France lost half of its farmers between 1982 and 1999; Germany has lost 25% of its farmers since 1995

These bare statistics only hint at the dramatic changes in farms across the developed world, as traditional family farms give way to agribusiness. In the 30 OECD countries (the world's richest), 1.5% of farms are lost every year, and with every farm lost, so a farmer leaves the land. In France, Germany, Belgium and Luxemburg, once renowned for their backbone of small farmers, 15 million people have left the land since 1957. In the UK, 80% of farms have disappeared since the 1950s. And America is faring no better. In the USA, the number of farms has shrunk from 6.5 million before the Second World War to less than 2 million today. And behind the stark figures lie many personal tragedies, and the loss of a rural way of life dating back through time immemorial.

As family farms go out of business, so land is concentrated into ever fewer and larger agribusinesses. Some think that this is the only way to achieve maximum farming efficiency, with economies of scale and a level of investment in heavy machinery and production facilities that only big farms can sustain. Without these, farms simply cannot compete in the global market. Supermarkets like dealing with large farms which can standardise production and deliver produce exactly as the supermarket wants, when it wants it, and at rock-bottom prices.

In fact, these rock-bottom prices are not necessarily coming from economies of scale. Almost two-thirds of the income of US farms actually comes from subsidies, and the situation is only slightly different in Europe. Indeed, large farms have become especially geared to reaping not food but farm subsidies. You might think that subsidies would go to the struggling small farmer. But 80% of the UK's £30 billion share of Europe's farm subsidies goes to the biggest 20% of farms. All this despite the fact that study after study has shown that small farms are more productive per hectare than large farms, not less. They are also better for employment, and less polluting. The vast, single-crop fields of agribusinesses are highly vulnerable to pests and diseases, and so demand huge inputs of pesticides and herbicides.

So why, then, are small farms disappearing so fast? The reasons are complex, but the main one is that farm-gate prices have shrunk to unmanageable levels, as processors and retailers take an ever larger share of food sold at ever lower prices in supermarkets. In Britain, farm-gate prices are now so low that farmers are paid less for most commodities than they cost to produce. In the USA, farm income halved in just three years between 1996 and 1999, and in 1998 pork was selling for barely a quarter of the farmer's break-even price.

If farming communities in the rich countries are under threat, so their counterparts elsewhere may be even worse off. In China, half the rural population has been forced off the land in the last twenty years, and 600 new cities will have to be built to accommodate all the displaced people, according to China's Vice Minister of Construction.

64. One of the fastest growing sectors in the food market is for so-called 'functional foods' or 'neutraceuticals'

After years of being bombarded with negative health messages telling them to cut this and reduce that, the consumer is ready, so the food industry believes, for a wave of positivity with foods that have added ingredients that will actually improve health. These foods with special health ingredients, called functional foods or neutraceuticals, cornered $16 billion in the USA alone in 2005 according to the market research group Leatherhead International.

Functional foods have been around for a long time. Iodine was added to salt, and vitamins added to milk over half a century ago to compensate for deficiencies in the diets of poor people. But it was in the 1990s that the idea of functional foods really began to take off.

Of course, all food is functional in some sense in that it contains ingredients that affect your health by providing nutrients, or simply calories. And many natural products are identified for their special health-giving ingredients such as calcium in milk and Omega-3 in oily fish. Moreover, the potential value of marketing food as functional has encouraged many food companies to simply shoehorn ingredients such as extra vitamins and minerals into existing products. Nonetheless, there are some genuinely new products with original functional ingredients, such as Yakult yoghurt with its *Lactobacillus casei Shirota* which promote 'friendly' bacteria in the gut, and Benecol margarine with the plant sterols that help reduce cholesterol.

More and more scientific research is being done to explore the relationship between diet and disease, and into particular substances that provide protection against particular ailments. However, the research is still in its infancy, and there are actually very few scientifically validated health claims that can be made. Among the exceptions seem to be the beneficial effects of probiotic yoghurts on the gut's bacteria.

One of the problems for governments is the way functional foods cross over between pharmaceuticals and food – and fall into a grey area for legislation. The three largest markets – Japan, the USA and the UK – all have regulations that permit foodmakers to make health claims for products in order to encourage healthy eating. But there is as yet little regulation to cover the validity of claims, or even to guarantee safety.

65. Blueberries may be more effective in protecting people against heart disease than statin drugs

For some time now, many people around the world have regularly been taking statin drugs to reduce blood cholesterol levels and lower their risk of heart disease. Indeed, statins are big pharmaceutical business, generating huge amounts of money for drug companies. Millions of apparently healthy people go into health centres to test the level of their blood cholesterol, and millions are recommended to start taking statin drugs if the tests show raised cholesterol levels. They will probably stay on the drugs for the rest of their life. Not all experts agree with the wisdom of this widespread statin attack, but those who take the drugs are convinced that it's the key to staying healthy.

In 2004, however, Dr Agnes Rimando, a researcher with the US Drug Administration, found that the common blueberry contains a compound called pterostilbene. This remarkable natural compound (pronounced 'ter-a-STILL-bean') may be able to lower blood cholesterol even more effectively than statins.

Rimando and other scientists had long suspected that the antioxidant chemicals in blueberries might help lower cholesterol – or rather the more dangerous LDL cholesterol. So she and her colleagues exposed four chemicals found in blueberries, including pterostilbene, to liver cells taken from rats – and found that pterostilbene activates a receptor that plays a role in lowering LDL and other fats in the blood.

Statins work in the same way, but are less specific and can

have side effects such as muscle pain and nausea. Because pterostilbene targets a specific receptor, it's likely to have fewer side effects. Indeed, since it's effective in even low concentrations, people might get the benefits by just eating blueberries. No one knows, yet, how many blueberries people would need to eat, but it adds to the growing list of health benefits which the tiny berry is being credited with. Its rich antioxidant content means that it's already a favourite with those who believe that antioxidants may help guard against the effects of ageing. Blueberries are also thought to help protect the body against cancer and diabetes – and even boost memory. As more and more people have come to know of the blueberry's power, so vast areas are being planted with blueberry bushes in places like Poland and California, as well as in traditional centres for blueberry-growing such as Maine.

66. 28 million Americans are at risk of osteoporosis because their diet is not rich enough in calcium

Because it comes on mainly in old age, most people think little of the threat of the bone disease osteoporosis. But because many of us are living longer, it's coming to affect more and more people. A crucial element in protection against osteoporosis is taking in sufficient calcium in your diet. Most experts recommend that this should be about 1,000mg a day – the equivalent of three servings of calcium-rich food such as milk, cheese, broccoli and sardines with bones. Yet according to a survey by the US Drug Administration, 8 out of 10 women and 6 out of 10 men have an intake that is less than three-quarters or even a half of the recommended dose. The risk of osteoporosis is exacerbated when this lack of calcium is combined with a lack of the vitamin D needed to absorb the calcium – usually obtained from sunlight – and also a lack of weight-bearing exercise.

67. The world produces and eats over 134 million tonnes of sugar a year

There's no doubt that the world has a very sweet tooth. The annual sugar production of 134 million tonnes means that we are growing enough sugar for every man, woman and child to consume over 30kg a year! That's a very big pile of sugar. It's called table sugar, but only a little is spooned directly into our tea and coffee, or sprinkled on our cereal. Most goes into processed foods. 70% comes from sugar cane, mostly grown in warm regions such as South America, India and China, and 30% from beet grown in cooler regions such as Europe and parts of the USA.

And that's not the only sugar we get. Table sugar or sucrose is only one of the many types of sugar, each with varying degrees of sweetness. The sweetest is fructose, which is found in fruit and honey. Then comes sucrose, then glucose, found in honey, fruit and vegetables; then maltose from grains and lactose from milk. Nutritionists sometimes talk about 'intrinsic' sugars, the sugars which occur naturally in food such as fruit and vegetables. 'Extrinsic' sugars are the ones we add to food.

In the past, the main concern about eating too much sugar was the damage it does to teeth by promoting tooth decay. However, experts are now increasingly concerned by its role in diabetes and obesity. In 2003, the World Health Organization and the Food and Agriculture Organization commissioned a report from 30 international experts. They concluded that sugars in all forms – not just table sugar and sugar added to foods, but all intrinsic sugars too – should amount to no more than 10% of the total energy intake in a healthy diet.

Many people believe eating too much sugar causes hyperactivity in children, and words like 'sugar rush' are now commonplace. But the scientific evidence for this is actually rather scant.

68. In the 1950s, around 60% of the cost of food in the shops went to the farmers. Now it's less than 9%

There's no doubt that food is big business, the world's biggest but for oil. The last twenty years have seen food retailing and food processing becoming amazing money-making enterprises, with companies such as Wal-Mart, Tesco and Nestlé regularly recording profits that dwarf the national products of many a medium-sized nation. Yet at the same time, surprisingly, farmers in the rich countries are in crisis, slipping into bankruptcy by the score, despite subsidisation on a massive scale. And in the developing countries, farmers are barely able to grow enough food to feed people.

Why then, in this time of booming global food sales, are those that actually produce it suffering so? The main reason seems to be that they are getting a much, much smaller proportion of the sale price of food than they did. In the UK, for instance, farmers get less than 9 pence for every £1 of food sold in the shops, whereas in the 1950s they used to get 50–60 pence. That massive lost share has gone to the big supermarkets and the food processing companies.

As the supermarkets and food processing companies have grown in size, they have cornered more and more of the food market. A third of all the food sold in the world is now sold through just 30 supermarket chains. In her book *Not on the Label*, Felicity Lawrence includes a diagram of the food business in Europe, drawn by food industry consultant Jan-Willem

Grievink. This revealing diagram shows the 160 million ordinary people who buy food at one end, and the 3.2 million European farmers who grow it at the other end – and in between the mere 110 buying desks of the food retailers who decide entirely what price to pay the farmers and what food to supply the consumers with.

This phenomenal concentration of buying power in the hands of just a few people means that farmers and suppliers have almost no power to set the prices they sell at. With few other outlets, suppliers have to accept the price offered by the supermarkets or processors, or go out of business. Indeed, suppliers frequently enter into bidding wars to court supermarket business, slashing their prices to the point where farmers are producing at a loss – sustained only by subsidies in the richer countries, and not at all in the developing world.

69. 97% of English meadows, 60% of ancient woodland and 20,000 miles of traditional hedgerow have been lost since 1950

Before the Second World War, farms in the developed countries were largely small and mixed, with farmers raising both livestock and crops, and rotating fields to keep the soil fertile and minimise the chance of pests and disease getting a hold. Spending on fertilisers, pesticides and other chemicals was minimal; natural manure was quite enough to keep the soil rich. But over the last 50 years there has been a quiet revolution that has utterly transformed farming practice and the farming landscape.

Mixed family farms have gradually been replaced by giant agribusinesses. These concentrate on producing single crops in large fields where harvests can be mechanised, or on intensive livestock-rearing in which the animals are often housed and fed indoors to maintain complete control. The aim is not to sustain a way of living through the generations but to produce maximum yields each year. Mechanisation, monoculture and inputs such as feedstock for animals (the feeding of grazing animals with protein meals such as cereals and meat rather than allowing them to graze) and agrichemicals have boosted yields so dramatically that this whole process has been called the Green Revolution. Cows give twice as much milk as they did a generation ago, chickens grow twice as fast and wheat fields may yield three times as much grain as they once did. The result has been the glut of cheap food which has created everything from food mountains to the obesity epidemic.

But these high yields come at a cost. Maintaining soil fertility and controlling pests in monocultural farming has meant huge inputs of agrochemicals, while feeding high-yield livestock in feeding houses demands massive energy and food inputs. Indeed, farming is now a major contributor to global warming and, ironically, global food shortages. On a more local scale, the changes in farming have transformed the rural landscape beyond recognition. In the UK, 97% of traditional meadows, 60% of ancient woodland and 20,000 miles of hedgerow have vanished since 1950, to be replaced by vast open fields and wire fences. And as the rich patchwork of ancient farming landscapes has been obliterated, so the wildlife that relied on it has suffered.

Without the flower-rich meadows, the bumblebees and butter-flies that relied on them have gone into serious decline. Since 1960, the great yellow bumblebee has become extinct in England and the carder and the large garden bee have declined by 95%. The loss of hedgerows and woodland and the ploughing up of meadows has cut England's bird population by half, with such once-common birds as the corn bunting, skylark, tree sparrow, turtle dove and song thrush now in dramatic decline. There are now less than a quarter of the number of skylarks that there were just 30 years ago.

70. A pound of minced beef can contain the meat from up to 400 different cows

Ever since the discovery of mad cow disease or BSE, people have been understandably worried about the possibility of eating infected meat. Government agencies have been making strenuous efforts to make sure that BSE and other germs don't get into the beef we eat. There's every sign that the campaign to eliminate BSE, at least, has been partially successful, but there's no reason for complacency – and there are at least possibilities that other germs may contaminate the meat we consume. The problem is to do with changes in the way beef is produced, especially the minced beef used in hamburgers.

Most beef cattle may start life on ranches, but they soon move to gigantic feedlots where 100,000 or more cows are packed into a small area and fattened with grain and other less savoury food ready for slaughter. Eric Schlosser, author of the book *Fast Food Nation*, describes conditions on these feedlots as 'like living in a medieval city, in their own manure'. Often these feedlots are right next to huge slaughterhouses and meat-processing houses, where hundreds of cows are slaughtered every hour and then ground into minced beef in an almost continual process. The slaughter rate is so fast that mistakes can easily be made, and manure can get on the meat as the animal is eviscerated, and infect it. With this massive concentration, too, there are huge possibilities for cross-contamination, especially when all the meat is fed into a gigantic global meat-packaging system.

You might think that all the meat in a small hamburger might come from a single cow. Marion Nestle, Professor of Public Health at New York University, points out that in one study, the meat in a single pound of minced beef could be traced to 400 different cows reared in six different states in the USA. So the chances of traces of pathogens getting into each helping of meat are massively multiplied, while at the same time the difficulties of tracing any outbreak of disease back to its source are correspondingly large.

Aware of the public relations danger of any outbreak of food poisoning, fast food buyers like McDonald's make tough demands on the meat-packagers for testing meat for pathogens. Yet, of course, it's the demands of big buyers like these, too, that has helped lead to the rise of the industrial feedlots. Today, just four big corporations, such as Tysons, control 85% of the beef market.

71. Genetically modified rice could not only stop many people starving but could prevent half a million children a year going blind

The world's population is growing by almost 100 million a year, and over the next half century it will grow by 3 billion. Yet already millions starve each year or are made ill by lack of the right food, especially in the poor countries of Africa and Asia. Some scientists believe that GM technology could help feed the world.

Rice is one of the world's basic or 'staple' foods. Many people in Asia and Africa live mostly on rice, and it's thought that rice production will have to increase by nearly a third to keep pace with population growth. The biotech industry believes that the solution is to genetically modify rice to boost yields. Corn grows much bigger than rice, partly because it's better at taking carbon dioxide from the air. This means that it can make more of its own sugar food with the aid of sunlight. So biotech scientists have now taken corn's carbon dioxide uptake genes and inserted them in rice. Experimental crops showed rice yields up to a third higher than normal.

At the same time, scientists have been trying to create 'golden rice'. Golden rice gets its name because it contains genes for beta-carotene, the substance that makes carrots orange. Beta-carotene is important because it helps the body make vitamin A. Between 100 and 400 million children around the world suffer from lack of vitamin A, which makes many blind and can prove fatal (see Fact 90).

Billions of people around the world also suffer from the blood disease anaemia. So golden rice has been modified to give extra iron in three ways. First, fungus genes make an enzyme that eliminates phylate, a chemical in rice that stops the body taking up iron. Second, spinach genes make ferritin, which makes the rice store more iron. Third, bacteria genes make cysteine, a protein which helps the body take up iron.

There are still many problems with golden rice. One is that beta-carotene helps raise vitamin A levels only when people have plenty of fat in their diet. Of course, the poor people who are most lacking vitamin A often eat little or no fat. Scientists think that it's a step in the right direction, but there has been so much opposition to the idea that at present golden rice is on hold.

One of the objections is that much of the technology is in the hands of a few big multinational companies. Many anti-GM rice campaigners feel that poor farmers could be locked into buying expensive seeds from the companies. These same farmers might also have to buy the pesticides and herbicides that work with GM products alone. The multinational companies would then gain enormous power over their lives. Small farmers who chose not to go along with this might be forced off the land by the few big farms who could afford to pay for the technology.

72. A typical family throws away 30–50kg of food packaging every month

Everyone knows that our food is over-packaged. Long gone are the days when fresh produce was tipped loose into a shopping basket, or at best contained in a brown paper bag. Now most food products are shrink-wrapped, encased in moulded plastic, and boxed up in multiple layers of colourfully printed paper and card. Even nuts and root vegetables come in one or two layers of packaging. Packaging accounts for a quarter of all household waste, and the vast majority of that is food packaging.

In 2006, journalists from the UK's *Observer* newspaper decided to monitor four typical families to see how much packaging they bought and threw away over a month. The answer was truly shocking. In the families' rubbish, they found up to 42kg of packaging alone. But this figure was more than doubled when you included what experts call the packaging's 'overburden' or ecological rucksack – in other words, the amount of material that goes to waste as the packaging is made. This doesn't even include the energy that goes into creating the packaging.

Food retailers sometimes insist that all this food packaging is entirely for the customer's benefit. Packaging, they say, is what keeps food in tip-top condition ready for us to eat. It certainly looks that way when you see brightly coloured, perfect looking vegetables in their hermetically sealed plastic armour, and it's at least partially true. But it can also sometimes be an illusion. In 2003, the Rome Institute of Food and Nutrition made a revealing discovery about the modified-atmosphere packaging (MAP) in which lettuces are often wrapped, for instance. The MAP kept the lettuce looking crisp and fresh, but it was as devoid of nutrients after three days as a limp lettuce stored in the open (see also Fact 78).

What packaging does do is allow retailers and suppliers to transport food simply and easily over large distances, and stack it up, price it and date it, ready to be whipped out on to shelves when needed. Packaging is also free advertising, and a come-on sign to the customer which also happens to give the 'value-added' impression which helps bump up prices and profits.

The big change in packaging is that it has become much lighter. Cans are made with much thinner metal than in the past, and heavy glass containers have been replaced with lightweight plastic. So the weight of packaging in relation to the weight of the food has come down dramatically. The problem is that while glass and metal, and to a lesser extent paper, is highly recyclable, there are real problems with recycling plastic.

The huge amount of oil that goes into plastic packaging, and the vast areas of landfill needed to take all the waste, have meant that many authorities around the world have introduced measures to make plastic food containers degradable or recyclable, and supermarkets, responding to the mood, have often introduced degradable or recyclable products of their own accord. Yet food still generates more waste than nearly every other sector of industry – over 4.6 million tonnes a year in the UK alone.

73. 60% of all food on supermarket shelves probably contains soya

The rise of soya has been one of the big unsung stories of the food industry. A bean, like broad beans and runner beans, soya was cultivated in China over 5,000 years ago. But until 60 years ago, few people in the West knew much about it, let alone ate it or grew it. Now it's one of the world's key food crops. Not only does soya contribute the vast bulk of feeds for livestock, it's also an ingredient in almost two-thirds of all processed food sold in countries like the UK. Variously labelled as soya protein, hydrolysed vegetable protein, tvp, lecithin and much more besides, it appears in everything from breakfast cereals and biscuits to noodles, soups and ready meals.

Soya's meteoric rise began after the Second World War, when German scientists found a way to get rid of soya oil's foul smell and taste. Subsidised and promoted heavily by the US government, American soya became a crucial part of the Marshall Plan for the reconstruction of Europe. Soya soon became the dominant feedstock for animals. From the 1960s on, soya has been widely used in processed foods and its rise has been unstoppable. In 1965, world soya production was 30 million tonnes a year. By 2005, it had reached 270 million tonnes, and it's still rising.

Up until 2003, it was the USA that led the way with soya. Still subsidised to the tune of billions of dollars a year, American soya farmers exported their product around the world in huge quantities. But in recent years, America has been overtaken by the massive expansion of soya production in South America – especially Brazil and Argentina. And the growth here is accelerating, prompting tremendous fears over the environmental consequences. It's estimated that an area of the Amazon the size of Britain could be cleared to make way for soya production by 2020. The worries are severe enough for even McDonald's to issue a statement asking its suppliers not to feed its poultry on Amazon soya.

In the 1990s, soya was promoted as a healthy option. Soya milk in particular was advocated as the wholesome vegetarian alternative to dairy milk, and the perfect source of calcium and protein for those who are lactose intolerant. Indeed, in the USA, 30–40% of babies are raised on soya milk as a matter of course. But in recent years, real doubts have been raised about just how healthy soya is. In traditional Asian cooking, soy sauce is made with long fermentation which reduces plant oestrogens and other ingredients that work against nutrition, such as phytates that block the enzymes that our bodies need to digest protein. Modern fast soya processing methods cut out this long fermentation, so the oestrogens and anti-nutrients are left in place.

Some scientists now believe that all these soya hormones could be harmful. In 2005, one scientist's research suggested that women hoping to get pregnant should avoid soya. Other research suggests that soya may interfere with testosterone levels. And a report by the UK Royal Society concluded that soya milk should not be recommended for infants, even if they had a dairy milk allergy.

74. The average American consumes 3,699 calories of food energy a day

Food energy consumption varies widely around the world. As you might expect, it's pretty high in European countries – typically well over 3,250 calories per person a day. But it reaches its peak in the USA, where the average person is eating almost 3,700 calories a day. That's considerably more than twice what they eat in countries like Somalia, where average daily consumption is less than 1,600 calories per person and most people have much less. Whereas a huge proportion of people are overweight in the developed world, over half of all children are considered underweight in India.

In the UK, the government issues Guideline Daily Amounts (GDAs) recommending daily intakes for energy, fats and saturated fats suitable for average adults over eighteen. GDAs recommend that women eat 2,000 calories of energy, 70g of fat and 20g of saturated fats, and that men eat 2,500 calories of energy, 95g of fat and 30g of saturated fat. So the average person in the developed world is eating 30–60% more energy food than they need. No wonder, then, that obesity is a growing problem. In the Third World, however, the average person is eating 30–50% less than they need, which is why of course so many suffer from malnutrition.

75. Almost 10 million live cows, 17 million pigs and 18 million sheep are transported around the world every year

The trade in live farm animals is much bigger than you might think. Cattle, pigs and sheep are herded into trucks, trains and ships in vast numbers and shipped off over huge distances. Every week, for instance, over 100,000 sheep are sent off from Australia alone. Many of them are bound for the Middle East, ready for slaughter in accordance with halal procedures. Saudi Arabia alone imports almost 5 million live sheep for slaughter in this way each year.

Despite stringent regulations to ensure the welfare of animals in transit, there have been many doubts about whether live animals should be transported long distances at all. Over 2,000 of the sheep leaving Australia for the Middle East each week, according Erik Millstone and Tim Lang's *Atlas of Food*, will die of disease and injuries sustained en route. The animals will be in transit for a month or more, travelling for days across land in Australia to reach a port, then spending three weeks crammed into the hold of a ship in near-darkness, and then left in a feedlot awaiting slaughter.

Although the shipping of live animals to the Middle East for halal slaughter is by far the biggest element of the trade in livestock, there is considerable movement of live animals on land as well. Within the USA, animals are often carried by road for thousands of miles from where they are reared to where they are fattened and slaughtered. In Europe, 2 million live pigs, cattle, sheep and horses are taken on long journeys each year, and 1.5 million pigs are transported from the Netherlands to Spain for fattening and slaughtering. Journeys from the north to the south of Europe can last 40 or 50 hours, all of which time the animals are packed into the same truck.

Opponents of the trade in livestock believe that live animals should never be transported. The animals should, they say, always be slaughtered near where they are reared and only the meat transported. Transporting live animals is also much more expensive than transporting meat. But there is a premium on 'home-killed' meat in France that makes it worth the cost. Moreover, slaughterhouses need to stay busy at times outside the local breeding season, and importing live animals may be the only way to do this.

76. If a meat-packing plant has surplus meat at the end of the day, it can put a new use-by date on the pack and send it out the next day

In these days of pre-packed and preserved food, there are often no obvious clues to lack of freshness, like the smell of meat or the browning of fruit. Instead, we have to rely on the use-by and best-before dates marked on the pack. But these are not always as reassuringly reliable as they seem, and they can be confusing.

In British supermarkets, for instance, food may be marked with 'use-by' dates, 'best-before' dates, 'sell-by' and 'display until' dates. Buyers often assume they mean much the same thing. In fact, they are very different. 'Sell-by' and 'display until' dates are not for the customer at all. They simply show shop staff when they need to restock or reduce the price of an item. 'Best-before' dates are for the benefit of the customer, and mean what they say. They are only guidelines to tell you when the food will be at its best. They are applied to foods that can safely be kept for some time without any health risk. Once the best-before date has expired, eating the food is not likely to do you any harm; it simply won't be at its best. It's actually quite legal for a shop to sell food past its best-before date, as long as it's fit for human consumption.

'Use-by' dates, however, have legal force and are applied to food that's highly perishable and could cause food poisoning if kept too long. Meat, fish, ready meals, dairy products and fresh juices must usually have a use-by date if they are sold packaged. They don't have to if they are sold loose, though. There may also be additional instructions, such as 'consume within one day of opening'. It's unsafe to eat food or drink past its use-by date even if it smells and looks fine (unless it was frozen in plenty of time).

Surprisingly, there are no hard and fast rules about deciding use-by dates. It's entirely up to those selling the food and applying the labels to decide how long the food will last, and estimates can vary. However, it's not in supermarkets' interests to poison their customers. Moreover, they can be prosecuted if there are any bad failures. So when the dates are in the supermarkets' control, they are genuinely fairly reliable – although with such vast operations there's always the possibility of mistakes.

Problems are more likely to occur with packagers. It's illegal for supermarkets to sell food past its use-by date. It's also illegal for them to alter use-by dates so that it can be sold for longer. This is not so for meat packagers. It's actually entirely legal for a chicken-processing plant, for instance, to re-package and re-date raw chicken and pass it off as fresh to the shops they sell to. According to the trade union Unison, such re-dating is common practice. The worry is that once a processing plant starts to re-date surplus chicken at the end of the day, it can quickly get out of control. Chicken could be re-dated again and again without anyone being aware of it.

77. The B vitamins are vital for the health of the brain

The B vitamins are also sometimes called the thinking and feeling nutrients because they play such a vital role in nourishing the nervous system. There are at least ten groups of them, and they work in keeping the communication between nerve cells up to speed. Many help form neurotransmitters. The vitamin B6 pyridoxine is central to the making of the neurotransmitters serotonin, dopamine and GABA. Vitamin B1, also known as thiamine, helps make the neurotransmitter acetylcholine, and when B1 is low, so are levels of the neurotransmitters glutamate and aspartate.

Shortages of B vitamins are linked to a lot of brain health problems. Prolonged B1 shortage can lead to psychosis, and maybe even reduced intelligence. B3 supplements can help migraines and headaches, and have been used to treat schizophrenia. B5 is sometimes known as the 'anti-stress vitamin', because of its role in controlling adrenalin. It's also thought to boost memory. But the B vitamin that excites especial interest when it comes to brain-ageing is B12, which helps form the myelin sheath that insulates nerves.

Various studies have shown that people with Alzheimer's typically have reduced B12 levels, while from the other end, other studies have shown that people with reduced B12 level are more likely to develop the disease. The evidence is growing that B12 might protect you against Alzheimer's. It may even boost your memory, though there's no hard evidence for that yet.

What is interesting is that as we get older, we lose some of our ability to absorb B12 from food – particularly if we use antacids a lot or drink frequently. One in 200 elderly people lack the gastric secretions necessary to absorb B12 altogether. If so, their doctor may recommend they take B12 injections to make up the deficit. Some doctors also recommend that adults over 50 eat food fortified with extra B12.

For most people, though, dietary B12 is enough. Indeed, upping the B12 content of your diet can be enough to reverse lapses in memory and slight problems with co-ordination and balance. Sometimes, this just means eating plenty of fish, offal, pork, eggs, cheese and milk. Because B12 needs folic acid to work well, it's also worth eating foods rich in folic acid such as bananas, oranges and lemons, green leafy vegetables and lentils.

- B1 (thiamine) – whole grain and enriched grain products like bread, rice, pasta, fortified cereals, pasta and pork

- B5 (panthothenic acid) – meat, poultry, fish, whole-grained cereals, legumes, milk, vegetables, fruit

- B6 (pyridoxine) – chicken, fish, pork, liver, kidney, plus whole-grain cereals, nuts and legumes

- B12 (cyanocobalamin) – eggs, meat, fish, poultry, milk and dairy products

- Folic acid – green leafy vegetables, bananas, oranges and lemons, fortified cereals, cantaloupe, strawberries and lentils

78. Pre-washed salads are typically washed in chlorine solution twenty times stronger than that in a swimming pool

Sales of salads in developed countries are almost double what they were a decade ago. It's not that we have become so enamoured with healthy, low-calorie living that we are actually eating that much more – rather that supermarkets have found a way of adding value to this simplest and freshest of foods, by providing it in pre-washed form. It seems a wonderfully convenient way of eating healthily.

When you see a salad inside its clear sealed plastic bag, you might think that the bag contains just air and salad. In fact, it's not air in the bag, but a modified form in which levels of oxygen have been reduced from the normal 21% to just 3% and carbon dioxide levels have been raised. Oyxgen is the gas that makes fruit and vegetables go brown and limp after they are picked. So reducing the oxygen keeps the salad fresh much longer. In fact, salads kept in this modified-atmosphere packaging (MAP) can stay looking fresh for up to a month.

Despite their apparent freshness, however, MAP wrapped salads may not be quite as healthy as they look. Research by Italian scientists at the Rome Institute of Food and Nutrition suggests that MAP packed lettuces lose many of their nutrients. Indeed, many of the antioxidant nutrients that make green salad vegetables good for health, such as vitamins C and E and polyphenols, all seem to be reduced. The problem is not that the MAP process actually robs salads of their nutrients; unwrapped salads also lose their nutrients quickly after they are picked. But you can tell the nutrients are gone in an unwrapped salad because it goes limp. With MAP, it stays looking fresh after its nutrient value has diminished.

The nutrient content of packed salad may be further reduced by the way it's washed. Supermarkets are very conscious of the possibility of food-poisoning from packaged salad. Because salads are typically neither cooked nor washed by consumers, they have to be free from contamination if they are not to cause outbreaks of *E. coli* or salmonella illnesses. Rather than take any risk of causing such an outbreak, supermarkets insist that their salads are carefully washed in what is effectively disinfectant. According to one food company boss, salads are typically soaked in a bath which contains 50mg of chlorine in every litre of water – that's twenty times the concentration of chlorine in an average swimming pool. Whether this heavy chlorination does anyone any harm no one knows, but many people think it at least kills some of the salad's taste.

79. The best way to stay young may be to eat less

It remains a controversial idea, but there is an increasing amount of evidence for the idea that eating less may be the most effective way to slow down ageing. The idea is that high-energy foods make the body burn out faster. By reducing the energy content of your diet, you let your body function more gently and more sustainably.

Scientists are not sure how 'caloric restriction' works, but experiments on mice show that it does. One recent study at Southern Illinois University showed that restricting calories has a similar effect on the body to knocking out the effect of growth hormones. The key seems to be insulin. Feed the body continually with a high-sugar diet and it adjusts by becoming less sensitive to insulin. Low insulin sensitivity means body cells begin to starve themselves of sugar (see Fact 49).

Moreover, some scientists believe that a high-energy diet, particularly an HFS (high-fat, high-sugar) diet typical of what we call junk food, helps generate chemicals in the body called free radicals. Free radicals play a key role in the ageing process by damaging cell membranes, proteins and DNA, the cell's master chemicals, through a process called oxidation (not dissimilar to rusting of metals). There is increasing evidence that restricting your calorie intake cuts the damage done by free radicals.

Interestingly, recent research suggests that a calorie-restricted diet could actually promote the growth of brain cells. This is because the lack of calories seems to put the brain under mild stress and stimulates cells to release a chemical called brain-derived neurotrophic factor (BDNF). BDNF is thought to be important in encouraging neurons to grow and make new connections.

Although the whole idea of caloric restriction is highly controversial, many experts now agree that most people can afford to cut down on their carbohydrate intake. It also makes sense to cut down on simple sugary food, especially refined sugar, and eat a balance of more complex carbohydrates, found in foods such as wholemeal bread, pasta, vegetables, pulses, brown rice and other grains. These are broken down in the body into glucose and other simple sugars slowly and steadily, to be used only as and when required.

80. The first GM food product was the Flavr-Savr tomato, which went on sale in 1994

The problem with tomatoes is that they go soft very quickly after they ripen. So normally, tomatoes are picked while they are still green. With luck, they will be ripe by the time they get to the shops, but by then they will have a very short shelf-life. In the early 1990s, scientists at the Californian biotech company Calgene realised that they go soft because of an enzyme called polygalacturonase (PG). The PG enzyme is released when the tomato ripens and softens it by breaking down cell walls. The Calgene scientists realised that if they could knock out the gene for the enzyme, they could make the tomato stay firm longer.

They worked out that by inserting a back-to-front copy of the PG gene into the tomato's DNA, they could neutralise it. Whenever the tomato made RNA copies of the PG gene, it would also make copies of the back-to-front gene. The PG RNA would then become entangled with the back-to-front PG RNA and so stop working. With this modification, the Flavr-Savr tomato could be left on the vine until it was perfectly ripe. It would still be ripe and fresh when it reached the shops.

The technology was very clever. Unfortunately, Calgene had made one fatal error. The strain of tomato they had chosen to modify was one of the most bland and tasteless. So although the Flavr-Savr was in wonderful condition when it was sold, it had no flavour to savour, and no one actually wanted to buy it.

The Flavr-Savr was launched in America with a media flurry as a scientific breakthrough. Not long after, it was quietly withdrawn as a commercial disaster. Naturally, food companies were wary for some time after of launching GM food products.

Interestingly, about the same time as the Flavr-Savr tomato was launched, some scientists were thinking of trying to put the genes of Arctic fish in plants. A fish called the Arctic flounder survives in icy waters because it makes an oil that stops water in its body freezing. Some scientists thought that if they could put the gene for this anti-freeze in plants, they might survive frosts better. It was only an idea, but newspapers mixed the story up with the Flavr-Savr tomato. So the myth spread that scientists were trying to put fish genes in tomatoes. People even began to think that the tomatoes would taste fishy.

81. A number of foods have been labelled 'superfoods' because of their supposed health benefits

In 1990, Barbara Griggs and Michael van Straten came up with the term 'superfoods'. Their idea was that 'a superfood is one with functional properties over and above the basic nutritional minerals and vitamins'. In other words, they are suggesting, certain foods contain special ingredients with health benefits over and above normal nutrition. Some may slow ageing. Others may reduce your risk of heart disease. Others may guard against cancer. And so on.

The idea has really caught on as scientific research focuses on chemicals in food that have particular effects on the body. The media love stories about superfoods because they are easy to understand and generate instant interest as they announce the latest miraculous research findings. Food retailers love the idea too, because they can add value to their products by making health claims about them.

However, many nutritionists are sceptical of the claims. In an article in *Which?* magazine, Professor Tom Saunders of London's King's College points out that 100 years ago digestive biscuits were being marketed as good for your digestion, while Coca-Cola was originally marketed as a tonic. He believes that the health benefits of superfoods are marginal, especially if not eaten as part of a good, balanced diet.

One of the problems is the speed with which new research is leaped on without real substantiation. In April 2006, newspapers reported that avocados contain chemicals called luteins, and luteins, it seems, may help prevent your eyesight deteriorating as you get older. Yet this claim was based on research in which elderly people with cataracts were given 15mg tablets of lutein three times a week. The lutein tablets did seem to reduce eyesight deterioration in those who took them. But to get the same amount of lutein from avocados, you'd have to eat maybe ten avocados a day.

Everyone seems to have their own top ten list of superfoods and it seems to change all the time, like the pop charts. But these items typically figure: pomegranates, oily fish, blueberries, broccoli, red wine, dark chocolate, avocados, green tea, oats, beans, spinach, yoghurt, organic milk.

Here are some of the superfoods, with some of their claimed benefits. Very few of these claims are thoroughly substantiated.

- Pomegranates: high in vitamin C and polyphenols, said to be antioxidants and so good at reducing cholesterol levels

- Oily fish: rich in the Omega-3 oils that are good for reducing the risk of heart disease and good for improving children's brainpower and concentration

- Red wine: contains antioxidants and in particular resveratrol, which is thought to thin the blood and reduce the effects of cholesterol

- Dark chocolate: contains flavanols/flavonoids, said to prevent blood clots and improve blood flow

- Blueberries: packed with vitamins C and E and potassium. Said to reduce diarrhoea, food poisoning, signs of ageing and blood pressure

- Broccoli: high in vitamins A, C and E and also a chemical called I3C thought to boost the body's ability to prevent cancer damage

- Yoghurt: said to fight bad bacteria in your gut, aid digestion and metabolise food. Also a good source of calcium and protein

- Walnuts: rich in Omega-3 oils and plant sterols thought to reduce cholesterol levels.

- Spinach: low in calories, high in vitamins B, C and E and antioxidants, plus iron and betaine, a vitamin-like nutrient thought to be good for your heart

- Oats: rich in cholesterol-lowering and digestion-improving fibre and minerals such as potassium and magnesium. Thought to lower cholesterol. Nutrients in oats apparently work better together than if consumed separately

- Beans: as rich in cholesterol-lowering and digestion-improving fibres as oats, high in vegetable protein, plus B vitamins and potassium

82. A cup or two of coffee daily can improve mental performance and alertness

Billions of people around the world now drink coffee and tea for the caffeine that helps them through the day. Caffeine is a psychoactive drug that in small quantities can lift your mood and make you mentally more alert. In bigger quantities, however, it can trigger anxiety, panic and insomnia. It can also cause headaches and raise blood pressure and cholesterol levels. Until recently, experts recommended that the ideal dose for raising mental alertness was one or two strong cups of coffee a day (100–200mg). However, recent research has shown that more may not do as much harm after all.

Nonetheless, tolerance to caffeine quickly builds up. Studies show that if you drink 400mg (4–5 cups) of coffee a day for just a week, caffeine no longer keeps you awake. Meanwhile, stopping your caffeine intake suddenly can cause withdrawal symptoms including headaches, irritability and tiredness lasting from one to five days, and typically peaking after 48 hours. Interestingly, caffeine increases the effectiveness of pain relievers in dealing with headaches by up to 40%, which is why many over-the-counter pain relievers include caffeine.

The caffeine content of coffee varies considerably. Dark-roast coffee, surprisingly, has less caffeine than light-roast because roasting takes out caffeine. And the stronger-flavoured Arabica has less than the common robusta. Typically, though, a single cup of instant coffee contains 65–100mg of caffeine, while an espresso shot contains 100mg and a cup of strong drip coffee contains 115–175mg. Decaf, by comparison, contains only about 3mg. Red Bull contains about 80mg, a can of Coca-Cola about 34mg, and a small chocolate bar about 31mg. Tea contains about half as much caffeine as coffee (30–60mg). But none of these figures is definitive. There's a huge variability in the caffeine content of a cup of tea or coffee prepared by the same person using the same ingredients and equipment day after day.

Besides caffeine, coffee and tea also contain another chemical – theophylline – which in drug form is good for asthma in relaxing bronchial muscle. Tea also contains another stimulant, theobromine. Theobromine's stimulant effect is milder but more lasting than caffeine's, and is the mood-enhancing chemical found in chocolate. So when someone says 'There's nothing like a good cup of tea for cheering you up', the effect is real, not imaginary.

83. Simply by eating, most of us are building up a store of toxic environmental chemicals in our bodies

In recent years a number of studies have revealed that most people have an array of toxic chemicals from the environment in their body. They are there only in tiny amounts, but they accumulate in body fat. The doses are generally so low that most experts believe there's no cause for alarm. However, we cannot be sure what the long-term effects of these chemicals are, nor what effect a cocktail of them might have.

One of the problems is that we humans are at the top of the food chain. Chemicals may be present only in small amounts in the environment, but they may get into the water supply, be ingested by fish, drawn up by plants, eaten by livestock and so on, then passed on up the food chain to humans. With each step the chemicals become more concentrated.

Organo-chlorine pesticides (OCPs) are now banned in the UK because of their toxic effects, linked to cancer, but they can remain in the environment for up to 50 years. Although the link is by no means proven, one recent survey revealed that patients with breast cancer were five times more likely to have the organo-chlorine pesticide DDT in their blood than healthy women.

Polychlorinated biphenyls (PCBs) were once widely used as coolants and lubricants. Like OCPs they are now banned, but can still leak into the environment from old buildings and so on. Then they can enter the food chain via small organisms and fish.

Research suggests that babies who feed on breast milk contaminated with PCBs can be slow developers, while girls exposed to high levels of PCBs become more masculine in their play.

Some plastic used for wrapping meat and dairy products contains phthalates. Phthalates may cause genital abnormalities in baby boys. Brominated flame retardants often used to make everything from carpets to computer screens fireproof can turn to dust, and, even if not breathed in directly, can settle on exposed food. They are thought to become concentrated in breast milk and disrupt the development of a baby's nervous system. Perfluorinated chemicals (PFCs) such as PFOA, often used in fast food packaging (as well as non-stick pans and floor waxes), can damage the immune system and cause birth defects.

In a recent test of food samples from supermarkets across the EU, the World Wildlife Fund found 'potentially harmful synthetic chemicals in all of the analysed samples, ranging from phthalates in olive oil, cheeses and meats, banned organochlorine pesticides in fish and reindeer meat, artificial musks and organotins in fish, and flame retardants in meats and cheeses'. Sandra Jen, Director of WWF's DetoX Campaign, commented: 'It is shocking to see that even a healthy diet leads to the uptake of so many contaminants.'

84. Over four-fifths of the world's grain is marketed by just three large American corporations

One of the most dramatic but silent shifts in the production of food over the last century has been the concentration of processing into the hands of a few global giants. Not so long ago, food production was a small-scale local business. Indeed, a huge proportion of people grew their own food. But with industrialisation in the 19th century, specialist food processors began to emerge, seeing an opportunity in the economies of scale possible with new technologies and mass markets. Steel roller mills, for instance, made previously exclusive white bread available to huge numbers of comparatively poor people. High-speed steel rollers pulverised the grain to make flour much, much faster and more cheaply than the old stone grinders.

Throughout the last century, more and more food has become processed so that very few products now arrive at the shop exactly as they came from the farm, even if the only addition is packaging. And as food has become increasingly processed, so it has come under the sway of a few large corporations who have grown bigger and bigger by mergers and acquisitions, and are still growing.

The biggest of the global food companies is Nestlé, with an annual income of $91 billion in 2005 and a fearsome domination of the global market in coffee and confectionery. Quite a long way behind comes Kraft, with an income of $31 billion. Then come a raft of others, each with an extraordinary degree of control in their own particular field – yet very few of these names are known to the public.

Tyson Foods is an American corporation based in Springdale, Arkansas. It's by far the world's largest processor and seller of chicken, beef and pork. Tyson alone processes over 8 billion pounds of chicken a year – that's 1,000 chickens every second of the day and night. Con Agra is pretty big too, worth $20 billion a year, dominating the meat industry like Tyson but also having a huge stake in the grain market.

However, the really big players in the grain market are Cargill, Arthur Daniels Midland and Louis Dreyfus. They control 80% of the world's grain – most people's staple food. Yet few outside the business have even heard of them. It's these companies that have pushed for market liberalisation to secure a giant global grain market, unrestricted by trade barriers. They are often behind the push for GM crops, too, which give them control over the grain trade from seed to flour. Cargill and the GM giant Monsanto work closely together.

85. On average, people in the UK eat out at least once a day

All over the world, there has been a tremendous move towards eating out rather than at home. This is partly because of increased availability and long working hours, but also increased affluence which allows people to, effectively, pay people to cook for them rather than cook for themselves. In fact, 80% of affluent professionals eat out regularly.

This doesn't necessarily mean that people are going to restaurants for full meals. In the UK, for instance, the biggest growth has been in take-out food, especially packed sandwiches, burgers, wraps and kebabs. In the UK, people eat out more than anywhere else in the world, averaging 365 'core meals' a year, according to the market analysis group Datamonitor. Italy comes second with 308, and the USA close behind in third place with 306 a year. But a great deal of the UK's spending is on cheap take-out food. In fact, a quarter of the money that people in the UK spend on eating out is spent on fast food. So while Britons eat out more than anyone, they actually spend less on doing so.

One reason for this is that Britons want to have their lunch on the go or at their desks rather than going for sit-down meals in restaurants. That's why the packed sandwich has been the biggest growth sector. Like people in many Mediterranean countries, however, Italians lunch at length in restaurants. The result is that they spend more on eating out than even the British – £1,265 on average each a year, compared with £1,224 in the UK. However, a new phenomenon in the UK is changing this picture – the pub-restaurant. According to a recent survey, 72% of adults were identified as users of pub-restaurants – in other words, nearly every one who can actually get to one. Other fast-casual eating places such as Spanish tapas bars and Japanese sushi bars are growing rapidly, both in the UK and USA, and are expected to do so elsewhere.

The total value of the market for eating out is gigantic. In the UK alone it's worth almost £90 billion pounds a year. The US market is worth three times as much. And it's growing. Data-monitor estimate that the total spent on eating in Europe and the USA will be a staggering $700 billion a year. In true business jargon, they also estimate that Europeans will have 12.9 billion extra 'out-of-home meal occasions' in 2009 compared to 2004. Americans will eat 8.8 billion more of these special meals. Europeans will also undergo another 6 billion 'snacking occasions', while Americans will enjoy an extra 7 billion. Home cooking and our hands-on knowledge of what goes into food will be almost totally eclipsed.

86. Deficiencies in essential acids in the diet can cause health problems

The essential acids are amino acids that the body needs to build proteins which it cannot make itself and so has to get from food. They include tryptophan, lysine, methionine, phenylalanine, threonine, valine, leucine and isoleucine. The body needs different amounts of these at different times, and a deficiency in any one at the wrong time can cause problems.

Young children need more tryptophan than adults, for instance, to make sure their bodies grow well and normally. The body uses tryptophan to manufacture many important substances. One is serotonin, used in the brain to transmit signals. Adults with too little tryptophan in their diet may become depressed, as their brains can't make enough serotonin.

Lysine isn't found in cereals, so people who depend solely on cereal for food can become ill through lysine deficiency. Methionine contains sulphur, vital to healthy hair, skin and nails. Phenylalanine and leucine are important in haemoglobin, the substance that carries oxygen around the body in red blood cells. Threonine is important in muscle fibre, while valine is essential for proteins involved in the nervous system.

87. The sweetener aspartame can cause mental retardation in infants with phenylketonuria (PKU)

When the sugar substitute aspartame was first introduced, it was hailed as a wonder by dieters who had long put up with the unpleasant aftertaste of saccharine. But aspartame, marketed as NutraSweet and Equal, is not entirely without problems. One in 20,000 babies, for instance, is born with phenylketonuria, the inability to metabolise the amino acid phenylalanine. Phenylalanine is one of the two amino acids in aspartame. So if infants suffering PKU are fed food containing aspartame, toxic levels of phenylalanine could build up in their blood. The result may be to cause mental retardation. Infants with PKU are placed on a special diet to avoid phenylalanine, while women diagnosed with PKU must avoid phenylalanine throughout pregnancy to avoid damaging the foetus. In the USA, aspartame-containing foods must state 'Phenylketonurics: Contains Phenylalanine'.

Back in the 1970s, a study suggested that aspartame caused brain tumours in rats, and ever since scientists have been trying to prove or disprove the dangers of aspartame. In 2005, a study suggested that very low doses of aspartame caused lymphomas and leukaemias in female rats. The European Food Agency, however, reviewed the study and concluded that any cancer link was simply a matter of chance. Then a study by the National Cancer Institute in 2006 showed there was no evidence that aspartame posed any cancer risk in elderly people, as had been feared.

However, the study was not controlled, nor did it include people who had been consuming aspartame over a lifetime. So the jury is out.

88. Most bread is now at least 45% water

In some parts of the world, bread is made as it has been for thousands of years, and in countries like France, craft bakery is a fiercely protected tradition. Nonetheless, there's no doubt that bread-making in the developed countries has become a much more industrial process. In the UK, now, 81% of all the country's bread is made by eleven companies in 57 factories, and just two companies, British Bakeries and Allied Bakers, make not far short of 70% between them. All but a tiny fraction of the rest is made by supermarket in-store bakeries using pre-baked or pre-mixed ingredients.

The result is that industrial processes like the Chorleywood bread process (CBP) have become widely adopted. Instead of allowing the dough to ferment and rise for a few hours, the CBP gets air and water in almost instantly using high-speed mixers. So the whole process is much, much faster and much more automated, which keeps the price of everyday bread very low. But it calls for extra yeast and chemical oxidants to get the air in, and harder fat to maintain the structure.

Until recently, the hard fat used in industrially-made bread was usually the tough, hydrogenated trans-fats. Because of all the bad publicity regarding the health risks of trans-fats (see Fact 29), some industrial bread-makers are replacing them with palm oils, but palm oils may turn out to be just as bad.

Another difference between industrial and traditional bread is the water content, which has always varied between bread types. Many Italian breads, for instance, have a very high water and olive oil content to give them their desirable soft, almost soggy texture. But over the last few decades the water content in standard industrially-made bread has gone up steadily. Extra water not only means a significant saving in flour costs, but means the soft dough can be achieved with tough, lower-grade flour. Otherwise you have to use higher-grade flour for the soft bread that most consumers like. Getting this extra water in was easy with chlorinated 'bleached' flours, but these were banned in 1998 in the UK for health reasons. Now many bread-makers achieve the same with GMO (genetically modified) enzymes.

Low-grade flour, higher water content, trans-fats (plus GMO enzymes or bleached flour) – all mean that the bread you buy in supermarkets may be just a bit less nutritious than you might imagine. In fact, in large quantities it could even be a health risk because of its high salt content. In the past, normal fermentation was quite enough to give bread a good flavour. The drastic cut in fermentation times in industrial processes means extra salt has to be added to stop the bread tasting like cardboard. According to some estimates, bread is now the biggest source of salt in the average diet – and that high salt intake brings attendant health risks (see Fact 34).

89. 'People who eat organic foods are eight times more likely to be attacked by the deadly new *E. coli* bacteria'

This is not a fact at all, but one of the many assertions by the fervent American campaigner against organic farming, Dennis Avery. A former government official during the Reagan era and author of the book *Saving the Planet with Pesticides and Plastic*, Avery has become a powerful voice for the agribusiness lobby. He argues that global warming is good because the warmth will help farmers, and that factory farms are environmentally friendly because they save space. His main target, though, is organic farming.

He is the originator of the myth, still often cited, that *E. coli* poisoning is a real risk for people who eat organic food. In an article in *American Outlook* in 1998, Avery began: 'According to recent data compiled by the US Centers for Disease Control (CDC), people who eat organic and natural foods are eight times as likely to be attacked by a deadly new strain of *E. coli* bacteria (0157:H7).' The CDC immediately stated that this was 'absolutely not true', but newspaper articles have since appeared across the USA and Europe perpetuating the myth of killer organic food. There is no substantial evidence at all that organic food is more likely to cause food poisoning.

Avery has put forward another argument against organic farming which has been widely taken up – that it uses up too much land and destroys wildlife habitat. He insists that if it were widely adopted it would cause an environmental catastrophe and mass starvation. He claims that 'selfish' organic consumers and farmers would rather watch millions of poor people in the Third World starve than let agribusiness save the day.

This claim merits some attention, but so far scientific studies have not backed it up in any way. For instance, Avery makes the assumption that without the extra fertilisers and pesticides, organic farming is bound to be much less productive than conventional methods. A detailed study published by Cornell University in 2005 showed that organic corn and soyabean yields were similar to conventional yields – only they used much less energy and were pesticide-free. Other studies show much the same. When it comes to meat farming, organic cannot compete with industrial farming for sheer productivity, but those in favour of organic farming argue that a shift away from meat production would redress the balance. One problem that organic farming cannot solve is the need for nitrogen. When crops are harvested, they take with them much of the nitrogen from the soil. If soil fertility is not to decline, nitrogen loss is made up for by applying artificial fertilisers. Organic farms replace it by manuring the soil. This works well while organic farming is small-scale, but no one knows how it would work on a large scale, or where all the manure would come from.

90. A simple lack of vitamin A makes tens of thousands of children go blind each year

I n countries where vitamin deficiency is easily rectified, it's hard to imagine that a simple lack of just one common vitamin can have such dire consequences. Yet over 100 million children in poorer countries suffer from vitamin A deficiency – and so are at risk of losing their sight. Already a quarter of a million children have been blinded this way, and the number is rising all the time. Going blind anywhere is a terrible affliction, but in poor countries it can be devastating. 90% of children who are blind don't go to school, and according to the Sightsavers Organization, half die within two years of going blind.

Vitamin A plays a number of key roles in the body. It's important for normal cell division and growth, and is also involved in building up the mucous layers that protect the lining of the lungs and digestive system. That's why a lack of vitamin A can make people prone to infection. But vitamin A's effects are seen most clearly in the eye.

Vitamin A plays a key role in health of the retina, the array of light-sensitive cells at the back of the eye that turn what you see into electrical signals to send to your brain. It's also responsible for keeping the outside eye lubricated and protected. A short-term lack of vitamin A can reduce the ability to see at night. A continued lack causes the drying out and scarring of the outer eye. The scarring of the cornea can lead to blindness.

Because of the key role that vitamin A plays in the health of the retina, the main form is known as retinol. As with most vitamins, our body gets vitamin A from foods, and the main sources of retinol are animal products, especially full-fat dairy produce, eggs and liver. Our bodies can also get it indirectly by converting a substance called beta-carotene. Beta-carotene is the pigment that makes vegetables such as carrots, squashes and sweet potatoes their orangey yellow colour.

Our bodies don't need much vitamin A, especially retinol which the body can't easily get rid of. Indeed, an excess of retinol is poisonous, and may be particularly damaging to foetuses in early pregnancy – which is why doctors advise expectant mothers to cut down on liver. Excess beta-carotene is usually less of a problem – but even beta-carotene may be linked to cancer when taken in excess in synthetic form rather than in food.

For the children of the world's poor countries, excess vitamin A is rarely an issue. The problem is not just that they never get the dairy food and eggs that gives us most of our vitamin A in the form of retinol. Even when they do get beta-carotene in vegetables, the lack of fat in their diet means that their bodies are poorly equipped to convert it to vitamin A.

91. Half of the world's total food energy and a third of its protein comes from just three cereals: wheat, rice and maize

The world depends heavily on a few basic staple foods which provide most of its population with their basic energy and nutrients. Wheat, rice and maize not only provide half of all the world's food energy and a third of its protein, but provide the staple food for over four billion people – that is, two-thirds of the world's population. These staple foods are especially important in Third World countries. While cereals provide less than 30% of the calorie intake in North America, Europe and Australia, they provide over 70% in countries like Vietnam and Cambodia, Mali, Niger and Ethiopia. In these poor countries, other foods such as sugars and animal products barely figure in the diet.

Wheat and rice are short on some vitamins, minerals and essential fats, but they are high in energy and protein. Wheat and rice both provide around 350 calories of energy per 100g. Eating 800g of rice or wheat would more than meet the average adult's daily needs for energy and protein.

Around the world, more than half a billion tonnes of both wheat and rice are grown each year. Most rice is eaten by people, and the grains are cooked pretty much whole. At least a quarter of the wheat crop, however, is fed to livestock, while most of the rest is milled into flour to make bread, noodles and pasta. Over 70% of the world's maize crop is fed to animals, even though it's just as nutritious as rice and wheat.

Climate makes it hard to grow cereals in much of tropical

Africa and South America. Here the staples are roots and tubers, such as cassava, yams, cocoyam, taro and sweet potatoes. Cassava is the staple food for about half a billion people, eaten in such foods as tapioca, gari, fufu and farinha.

As countries develop, staples play a decreasingly important part in the diet. In the USA, for example, less than 20% of food energy comes from cereals. Almost as much comes each from sugar and sweeteners and fat. The picture is similar in Canada, Europe and Australia. In fact, most developing countries are now going through a 'nutrition transition'. In this, consumption of staples and other traditional crops such as pulses and oilseeds is declining, while the intake of fat, sugar, salt and meat is rising, along with the consumption of refined and processed foods.

92. Surveys of children's food show that a third contains azo dyes linked to asthma and hyperactivity

Azo dyes are added to food to create attractive colours. In fact, 60–70% of all the dyes used in foods are azo dyes. They can be used to create a huge range of colours, but most are yellow or red. Very few people, if any, are allergic to azo dyes directly. However, what they can do is stimulate the immune system to heighten its allergic reaction to other substances. One well-known azo dye, called tartrazine, is thought to heighten the allergic reactions that trigger asthma. Not all asthmatics are affected like this but it seems sensible for asthmatics, especially children, to steer clear of azo dyes. Since the 1970s, it has been thought that azo dyes may cause hyperactivity in children, but studies since then have been inconclusive. It may be that it affects certain children but not others. Foods that are likely to contain azo dyes include red, orange or yellow coloured juices, soft drinks, sweets, desserts, toppings, syrups and sauces.

93. A third of all food produced in the UK is simply thrown away

In a world where billions of people go hungry, the amount of food that is simply thrown away in the developed world is astonishing. The UK is the worst culprit, throwing away 30–40% of its food each year. Over 17 million tonnes of food worth up to £20 billion is simply chucked into landfill sites. What's amazing is that at least a quarter of this is perfectly edible as it goes into the hole. More than a third of it is thrown away by farmers because of fixed contracts with processors and retailers, which specify the size and shape of fruit and vegetables and the exact quantity required. A bumper crop year, for instance, doesn't necessarily mean extra food in the shops; it can simply mean that more of the crop is ploughed in or thrown away. Supermarkets have reduced the amount of food they waste through improved storage and distribution. All the same, UK supermarkets still dump more than half a million tonnes of food in landfill each year.

Yet it's households that are perhaps the most profligate with food. People typically throw away up to a third of the food they buy simply because they buy too much. A recent survey by Prudential Insurance showed that two-thirds of households throw away at least one bag of salad each week unopened, a perfectly good loaf of bread and fresh fruit. About half throw away milk, cheese and meat. Some estimates suggest that the average person throws out 2.7kg (6lb) of food a week. When London organisations began to set up food waste collection, they found that a third by weight of all household waste is food, much of which is completely edible. The UK is worst for waste, but the USA isn't far behind, as are many developed countries. One study by the University of Arizona suggested that 40–50% of all food ready for harvest in the USA never gets eaten.

94. The human body needs to take in small quantities of certain minerals regularly to stay healthy

Minerals help form the hard parts of the body (teeth and bones), but also play a key role in a huge range of other body processes, such as the permeability of cell membranes, the activity of muscles and nerves and blood volume. Indeed, minerals are as vital to the body as oxygen: it can go without vitamins for some time, but mineral deficiencies can quickly become life-threatening. Often apparently mystifying health problems can be traced to mineral deficiencies. Fortunately, a normal, well-balanced diet provides an adequate supply. These are good sources of the main minerals the body needs:

- Magnesium – whole grains, legumes, nuts, sesame seeds, dried figs

- Potassium – apricots, avocados, bananas, melons, grapefruit, kiwi fruit, oranges, strawberries, prunes, potatoes, pulses, meat, fish

- Calcium – milk and dairy products, fish with edible bones, sesame seeds

- Zinc – oysters, red meat, peanuts, sunflower seeds

- Selenium – meat and fish, dairy foods such as butter, brazil nuts, avocados, lentils

- Manganese – nuts, cereals, brown rice, pulses, wholegrain bread

- Copper – offal, shellfish such as oysters, nuts and seeds, mushrooms, cocoa

95. Sales of chicken have increased five-fold in the last twenty years

In the last twenty years, there has been what some people have called a Livestock Revolution. The number of farm animals on the planet has shot up hugely faster than the human population, as more and more people around the world have begun to eat meat on a regular basis. Increasing numbers of people are affluent enough to afford meat, and the rise of intensive 'industrial farming' has meant that animals can be raised to give meat very cheaply.

We are now eating much more meat of all kinds than we were less than two decades ago, but it's chicken consumption that has really gone up on an almost unimaginable scale. In places like North America, Europe, Brazil and Thailand, vast chicken factories churn them out for slaughter by the billion. Factory farming has made chicken so cheap that this meat, once considered an occasional luxury, is one of the cheapest of all forms of protein. A whole chicken can be bought for the price of a pint of beer or less.

Part of the reason for the rise in chicken consumption is its use in brand-name convenience foods and fast foods. In the early 1980s, McDonald's Chicken McNuggets revolutionised chicken as both a convenience and frozen food, while Kentucky Fried Chicken is now one of the biggest global fast-food brands, as popular in South East Asia under various franchises as it is in its American home. In the USA, almost half the chicken sold goes through food-service outlets, and two-thirds of this is through the well-known fast-food chains.

Another reason for the rise in chicken consumption has been changes in diet. This is partly because of health concerns. Weight for weight, chicken has much less fat, especially saturated fat, than beef, so is a much healthier option for those at risk of heart disease. The preference for chicken is also partly a matter of taste. Chicken is softer, easier to chew, and has little of the unpleasant greasiness and gristle of beef. It also mixes well with sauces and other ingredients in processed foods, so makes the perfect meat for ready meals. Although some say that it's bland-tasting, it's very blandness gives it tremendous appeal to kids, especially when given the tang of a barbecue or a frying in oil.

Yet there's no doubt that producing the huge number of chickens to satisfy the demand has its downsides, both in terms of the nutrition and safety of the food and the welfare of the birds (see Fact 36).

96. Many food crops have now been genetically engineered to be weedkiller-resistant

Weeds are particularly difficult for farmers to deal with. They grow in among their crops and compete with them. It's not as easy to kill weeds with chemicals as it is insect pests. This is because chemicals that kill all weeds could well damage the crops as well. So many farmers attack weeds with a range of different herbicides (plant killers), each one effective against a narrow range of plants. This is time-consuming and expensive.

The world's biggest-selling weedkiller is called Roundup, and is made by the giant American company Monsanto. Roundup is based on a chemical called glyophosphate. It's essentially harmless to animals, but kills nearly all plants. So farmers had to use it very carefully. If they were careless, Roundup might kill their crops as well as weeds.

In the early 1990s, gene scientists around the world began to look for a gene that would resist Roundup. A gene like this could be inserted into crop plants. Then the plants could be sprayed freely with Roundup. All the weeds would be killed, but the crops with the resistant gene would survive.

Monsanto's scientists led the search. The company's idea was to sell farmers both Roundup to kill all the weeds and special 'Roundup Ready' seeds for their crops – seeds with a gene that enabled them to resist Roundup.

In the end, it wasn't Monsanto's scientists who found the Roundup Ready gene. It was researchers at a small Californian company called Calgene in 1992. Calgene's researchers had the clever idea of looking for bacteria that grew in glyophosphate chemical dumps. If these bacteria could grow in glyophosphate dumps, they could clearly resist Roundup weedkiller.

Roundup Ready soyabeans were first planted in the USA in 1996. Within a year, a sixth of all America's soya crop was Roundup Ready. Soya was quickly followed by Roundup Ready cotton, corn, alfalfa and wheat. Since then, other companies have developed crops engineered to resist herbicides in the same way. The German company Hoechst, for instance, came up with LibertyLink crops engineered to resist the company's herbicide Basta (called Liberty in the USA).

One of the fears about giving crops genes to resist weed-killers was that the genes could spread to weeds. If the genes got into weeds, superweeds that are resistant to weedkillers could develop. Although no such weeds have appeared yet, GM genes were found to spread easily between different oilseed rape plants in Canada. GM crops planted in separate fields with different genes acquired the genes from their neighbours within a few years. Some campaigners believe that the only way to ensure that GM genes don't spread is to have a three-mile 'exclusion zone' around GM farms in which no similar plants are grown. This might just be possible in large countries like Canada, but is impossible in smaller countries like the UK.

97. Amino acids are the basic materials from which all living matter is made

More than 100 amino acids occur naturally, but just 22 of them combine to make the millions of different proteins which are so vital to life. When amino acids were first identified, scientists thought there were just twenty involved in the making of proteins. But in 1986, Ohio university scientists investigating microbes that produce natural gas discovered another. They called it selenocysteine. In 2002, the same group of scientists found a 22nd amino acid in a very ancient kind of bacterial-like microbe called Archaea. This acid they called pyrrolysine. Most scientists think a few more will be found as they study other microbes. All the same, these extra protein-making amino acids are rare, and it's the original twenty that are crucial in the proteins of the human body.

Proteins are some of the largest and most complex substances in the universe. There are thousands of different kinds in the human body, and they perform thousands of different tasks, from building structures such as hair and nails to controlling chemical reactions. Keratin, for instance, makes up nails and many other parts of the body, while haemoglobin transports oxygen through the blood in red blood cells. The simplest proteins are made up of just four different kinds of amino acids. Most of the more complex proteins are made from all twenty acids, however.

The human body uses up proteins all the time. They are lost through bodily waste, perspiration, the growth of hair and nails, and through many other processes. As a result, the body needs a regular supply of new proteins, and it needs amino acids to make them with. Green plants and some microbes can make all the amino acids they need. But humans and most other large animals can make only half of them. The ten or so amino acids that the human body can make for itself are called non-essential acids. The rest are called essential acids, and your body gets them from the food you eat.

When you eat food, you are often taking in ready-made proteins. But these proteins are not in a form that the body can use. To use them, the body must first break them down in the digestive system into the individual amino acids they are made from. The body's cells then re-assemble them to make the necessary proteins. Some foods are so rich in certain kinds of protein that they contain all the essential acids the body needs. These proteins are called complete proteins. Cheese, eggs, fish, meat and milk are packed with complete proteins.

Other foods contain what are called incomplete proteins, because they contain only some of the essential acids. Cereals, vegetables and nuts are rich in incomplete proteins. Although no single incomplete protein contains all the amino acids the body needs, a combination of them might do. Cereals alone might not provide all the right amino acids, but cereals combined with the right vegetables may do. This is why a balanced diet is so crucial to good health.

98. Food filled with chemicals that counter the effect of oxygen could slow down the ageing process

You can avoid cigarettes, alcohol, caffeine, fats and all the other things that are said to be bad for you. But you can't avoid oxygen – and this, some scientists say, is the chemical that ages you most surely. Oxygen is highly reactive, and that's what makes it so useful in the body. It's the vital element that helps body cells release energy from sugar. But as it does, it lets slip a little pollutant called a free radical, or oxidant, the same thing that makes iron rust. Every day countless free radicals are let loose in the cell, and they tumble out banging into cell membranes, proteins and, crucially, the cell's DNA, doing a little damage as they do. Some 10,000 free radicals strike the cell's DNA every day. Some are intercepted by antioxidant chemicals, and when they do get through, the DNA manages to repair itself with special proteins. Eventually however, some scientists think, the DNA's ability to fend off radicals and repair the damage becomes impaired. Sensing damage, the cell self-destructs, and so the ageing process gallops on.

So what if we used antioxidants – that is, chemicals that mopped up free radicals – to slow the process? It's certainly worked in experiments on fruit flies and rats. But there's no evidence, yet, that it will work in humans. Vitamins C and E are antioxidants, but there seems no proof that vitamin supplements will make much difference. For one thing, your body can absorb only so much of these vitamins; and for another, you get most of the basic antioxidants you need from your normal diet. It may be that there are antioxidant drugs you can take to boost your defences against free radicals, but no one yet knows what they are, or what their effects might be.

No one really knows whether eating food rich in antioxidants will help defend against the damage done by free radicals in your body cells – or even if it's worth defending against. But it certainly can't do any harm to eat more of the fruit and vegetables that are rich in antioxidants.

- Fruit: raspberries, strawberries, red grapes, oranges, plums, cherries, blueberries, kiwis, pink grapefruit, raisins, prunes

- Vegetables: corn, onions, red peppers, spinach, aubergine, sprouts, kale, broccoli, beetroot, alfalfa sprouts

99. The Glycaemic Index may give a better idea of how fattening a food is than calories alone

The Glycaemic Index, or GI, is a measure of how fast the carbohydrates that food contains are broken down and affect levels of glucose (sugar) in the blood. Pure glucose is given a GI of 100, and all other carbohydrates are compared with this. A food with a GI of under 55 has a low GI. Food low in GI tends to keep us feeling fuller for longer, helping to keep weight down. It also contributes less than high-GI food to heart disease and helps keep diabetes under control. GI labelling is widely used in Australia, and is being seen increasingly in other countries too.

The more processed a food is, the higher its GI tends to be, because, in effect, the processing partly digests the carbohydrate, making it easy for the body to finish the job and convert it into blood sugar. Breakfast cereals like cornflakes, for instance, have a high GI. In the same way, cooking can increase the GI of food, which is why long-baked potatoes have a higher GI than just boiled new potatoes. Fibre, however, tends to lower GI because it slows digestion down.

GI labelling can be misleading, though, to how fattening a food is – because it takes no account of just how rich in calories a food is. Crisps, for instance, have a relatively low GI of around 54, but the fat used to fry them is so rich in calories that they are actually a fattening food.

Lower-GI food	Higher-GI food
Breakfast cereals	
Porridge	Cornflakes
Sugar-free muesli	Sweetened muesli
Breads	
Granary	White bread
Rye bread	Brown bread
Rice and cereals	
Basmati rice	Long grain rice
Pasta	
Vegetables	
Boiled new potatoes	Mashed potatoes
Spinach, broccoli	Parsnips
Fruit	
Fresh fruit salad	Canned fruit salad
Medium-ripe banana	Over-ripe banana

100. Eating dark chocolate could be good for your heart

According to a recent study, eating a little dark chocolate every day could be good for you. Research at Johns Hopkins University in the USA found that cocoa beans have a similar biochemical effect to aspirin in reducing the likelihood of blood clots. The scientists estimate that eating a little dark chocolate every day could halve the risk of a heart attack. However, what they don't emphasise is that eating a lot of chocolate is actually bad for your heart, because even dark chocolate is jam-packed full of sugar and animal fats.

101. In future, meat may be grown in cubes in factories without ever becoming part of an animal

Stem cell technology has inspired scientists with all kinds of ideas for growing tissue independently. Stem cells are the basic body cells from which all others can grow. Scientists are already experimenting in the lab with growing new organs for transplant from stem cells on dissolvable matrices. Some scientists believe that meat can be grown in boxes from stem cells. Morris Benjamin of New York's Zymotech Enterprises has extracted stem cells from fish embryos and used them to grow fish muscle cells by stimulating them with a blend of electricity, hormones and nutrients. He has already grown a mass of fish muscle cells that looks, smells and even cooks like fish fingers. He thinks that one day he will be able to grow chunks of bonelesss chicken breast in the same way. Researchers at Utrecht University in the Netherlands are experimenting with pig stem cells to grow vats of pork to create a suitable pork mince for making into sausages and burgers.

The scientists argue that in this way they could make meat from pretty much any species you wanted, including rare and endangered species, without harming any animal, and without any of the diseases that live animals are prone to. Some argue that even vegetarians should have no problem eating this meat, since no animal would have to die to provide it.

Sources for the 101 Facts

One of the interesting things about compiling this book was finding out just how many people have axes to grind and agendas which encourage them to draw particular facts out and not others. It's certain that my choice of which points to dwell on, for instance, gives a spin that makes this book less than objective. However, I have tried as much as possible to evaluate sources and cross-check them wherever I felt there might be some undue bias involved. So very few of the facts come from a single source. What follows is a list of the key sources:

Books

A Consumer's Guide to Genetically Modified Food, Alan McHughen, Oxford University Press

DNA, James Watson, William Heinemann

Don't Eat this Book, Morgan Spurlock, Penguin

Fast Food Nation, Eric Schlosser, Penguin

Food For the Future, Colin Tudge, Dorling Kindersley

Not on the Label, Felicity Lawrence, Penguin

Nutrients A–Z, Dr Michael Sharon, Carlton

Shopped, Joanna Blythman, Harper Perennial

The Composition of Foods, R.A. McCance and E. Widdowson, Food Standards Agency

The Food System: A Guide, Geoff and Tony Worsley, Earthscan

The Science of Food, Gaman Sherrington, Butterworth Heinemann

You Are What You Eat, Kirsten Hartvug and Dr Nic Rowley, Piatkus

What Are You Really Eating?, Amanda Ursell, Hay House

The Truth About Food, Sir John Krebs, Royal Institution

Publications

New Scientist

Scientific American

The Guardian newspaper
The Independent newspaper
The New York Times newspaper
The Observer newspaper

Organisations

Australia Food Safety Campaign
Australian Government Department of Agriculture, Fisheries and
   Forestry (DAFF)
Consumers' Association (Which)
European Food Information Council (EUFIC)
Food and Agriculture Organization
Food and Drink Federation
Food Marketing Institute
Greenpeace
Institute of Food Research
McDonald's
Monsanto
Oxfam
Soil Association
Tesco
UK Food Standards Agency
UNESCO
United States Department of Agriculture
US Centres for Disease Control
USDA Food and Nutrition Information Center
USDA Food and Safety Inspection Service
Wal-Mart
World Health Organization
www.foodsafety.gov
www.Nutrition.gov

Index